MOBILITY AND CHANGE IN MODERN SOCIETY

Mobility and Change in Modern Society

Geoff Payne

Dean, Faculty of Social Science
Plymouth Polytechnic

© Geoff Payne 1987

First published 1987

Published by
THE MACMILLAN PRESS LTD
Houndmills, Basingstoke, Hampshire RG21 2XS
and London
Companies and representatives throughout the world

Typeset by Vine & Gorfin Ltd, Exmouth, Devon

Printed in Hong Kong

British Library Cataloguing in Publication Data
Payne, Geoff
Mobility and change in modern society.
1. Social mobility—Great Britain
2. Great Britain—Occupations
I. Title
305.5'0941   HN400.S65
ISBN 0-333-41825-6 (hardcover)
ISBN 0-333-41826-3 (paperback)

Contents

List of Tables

Acknowledgements

This book is one outcome of a large-scale piece of research which lasted for a number of years and involved literally hundreds of people, not least nearly 5000 Scots who provided the basic information about patterns of mobility. They cannot all be thanked by name, but there are several individuals who deserve particular mention. Mick Carter appointed me as Director of the Scottish Mobility Study, which furnished the empirical data and the experience on which this book is based. He was never less than completely fair and honest, and had the strength of character to let me go my own way and yet to back me up when the going got tough. More recently, Richard Brown's patient encouragement and careful criticisms of earlier drafts ensured that I eventually completed the project. Judy Payne not only carried out all the normally acknowledged duties of an author's spouse, but organised and ran computer runs at short notice – even in the middle of the night. Her contribution by way of support has been every bit as important as her sensible comments on some of my more hare-brained ideas.

Among other people involved, Graeme Ford and Catherine Robertson, the other original members of the Scottish Mobility Study team, worked very hard in the fieldwork stage. Graeme was a particularly stalwart aide in those early days: he cheerfully took on whatever work was needed, even when his splendidly agnostic turn-of-mind made him doubt its value. Robert Moore was another source of support in Aberdeen, while I am also grateful to the undergraduates and postgraduates (Tony Chapman in particular) at Plymouth Polytechnic whose work has continued to stimulate my interest in social mobility.

I have been fortunate to receive excellent secretarial support throughout my research, both in Aberdeen and Plymouth. Mae Lowe helped greatly by removing administrative burdens from me at key points, and was a further source of encouragement. The final preparation of the typescript was carried out by Jane Doughty, Dawn Cole and Carole Vincent with great tolerance and goodwill; indeed, all the office staff deserve my thanks for the way they shared the burden.

Some parts of this book have appeared as journal or conference papers: numerous readers and audiences have helped to clarify what I meant to say. As always, the author must take the blame for any remaining shortcomings. Part of Chapter 4 is taken from an article in *Sociological Review*, vol. 25, no. 1; Chapter 6 largely appeared in

Sociology, vol. 11, no. 2; and Chapter 7 combines material from articles in the *Scottish Journal of Sociology*, vol. 1, no. 1, and the *British Journal of Sociology*, vol. 34, no. 1. I am grateful to the respective editors and publishers for permission to reprint the substance of these articles.

The research was financed by a grant from the Social Science Research Council, while the writing of this book was made possible by a period of sabbatical leave from Plymouth Polytechnic which was spent at the Research Centre for the Social Sciences, Edinburgh University.

GEOFF PAYNE

Introduction

'Social' or 'class' mobility is normally thought of as a movement between social classes, whereas it is operationalised in occupational terms and what is actually measured is movement between broad groupings of occupations. It is therefore often forgotten that social mobility is in fact occupational mobility, and so it is a product of employment processes which have taken place in specific historical and economic circumstances. The sociological literature contains few attempts at an occupational explanation of social mobility or accounts of how changes in mobility in the class structure have been altered by many social and economic events like two world wars, or the Great Depression.

In order to gain a fuller understanding of mobility, and to return it to both mainstream sociology and the comprehension of the ordinary person in the street, mobility needs to be treated in a more concrete sense than in earlier studies, which have taken an interest in mobility only to the extent that it shed light on theories of stratification. An important step in achieving this is to understand how a number of theoretical perspectives have informed mobility analysis. The opening chapter therefore starts with a consideration of earlier key contributions, and attempts to show that mobility research has become increasingly restricted to a limited number of concerns. Sorokin's original multidimensional and all-encompassing vision has been replaced with more specific technical concerns about comparative analysis of how 'open' societies have become, or how national, educational and class recruitment systems operate. There are, however, a number of other links which can be made to wider sociological concerns. Conceiving of mobility in occupation terms makes it easier to see what such links would be like (for example, with labour market theory, occupational transition, or theories of post-industrial society).

That is not to say that mobility is not about stratification: indeed, quite the reverse. But before one can deal with the abstractions of mobility and class analysis, it is necessary to establish the occupational base on which a number of theoretical class models have (often unwittingly) been built. The present study concentrates more on this basic task as a necessary first step rather than theorising in detail on the current state of social class in Britain.

Central to the analysis of occupational mobility is the question of the

evolution of occupational structures. Put at its most simple, in modern
society an increasing proportion of jobs are white collar. This creates
new opportunities for both upward mobility and the 'inheritance' of
non-manual employment by the children of non-manual workers.
Mobility rates are therefore seen as directly related to the way in which
demand for labour in a society changes over time.

While it is a significant step to explain mobility in terms of occupational transition, and this itself is not without its problems, it is also
necessary to ask what brings about this increase in the proportion of white
collar jobs? Two alternative explanations are offered: on the one hand, a
Marxist view sees the conditions of production under monopoly
capitalism as the root cause, while on the other, the theory of industrial
society attributes occupational transition to new technologies and the
logic of industrialism. The former view also tends to play down the
significance of this structural change for class relations, whereas the
latter view places the new middle classes at the centre of the stage.

Much of Marxist writing on mobility and occupational change is
concentrated around two problems, the nature of the 'new middle
classes', and the deskilling of the labour process. Despite recent claims
to the contrary, Marx wrote very little on the new middle class or
mobility, and he did not see its importance. This is not surprising,
because he also failed to account adequately for the occupational strata
that lie between the bourgeoisie and manual labourers. Recent debates
(for example, the writings of Poulantzas, Hunt and Wright) are
reluctant testimony to the fact that while Marx recognised the existence
of the *dritte personen* he afforded them little attention. Nonetheless, it is
possible to identify within the organisation of monopoly capitalism
factors that generate new occupational roles: the banking system and
competitive exploitation of science for profit maximisation are two
examples. The discussion of the theory of capitalist society in Chapter 3
tries to assemble an explanation of why new occupations are created,
and also draws attention to what the incumbents of such occupations do
in the production process. The latter involves an analysis of
occupational functions which lies at the heart of arguments over
boundaries between the capitalist and the new middle classes on the one
hand, and the new middle classes and the class of manual labourers on
the other.

The second theme in Marxist accounts of the labour process is the
degradation of skills and the proletarianisation of marginal labour.
Although such views have recently come under attack, a further test of
such models is to examine flows of recruitment between occupational

classes with similar skill levels. Deskilling and proletarianisation are important for accounts of mobility because they propose that the genuine opportunities for mobility are increasingly restricted. In contrast, theories of industrial society (which are dealt with in Chapters 4 and 5) explicitly identify the upgrading of skill levels and increases in social mobility as core elements of advanced industrialisation. Because specialist abstract knowledge is central to the technology on which modern or post-industrial societies depend, new occupational roles are needed to acquire, apply, and coordinate that knowledge. The new middle classes that result are seen to be sufficiently numerous and influential to warrant a revision of traditional class theory. While some writers suggest that class conflict is replaced by a new social order, others regard class conflict as substantially modified by the existence of the new classes. It is the latter view that the present author finds more plausible, and the professional/managerial class is singled out as requiring particular attention in the empirical analysis. Not least, the relationship between occupational achievement and educational qualifications is identified as an important factor in recruitment to this class. Following Giddens and Parkin, credentialism and mobility are seen as central to an understanding of this class, although perhaps such an 'understanding' has yet to be achieved.

Three main themes from the theory of industrial society are regarded as particularly relevant to mobility research. The first is the idea of sectoral shift of employment from primary production and manufacture into service industries. This creates new kinds of occupations and reduces the level of employment in older types of occupation. Sectoral shift means occupational transition and therefore analysis by industrial sector is one of the major tools to be used in the investigation of mobility rates. Second, writers on modernisation and convergence have also claimed that mobility rates increase in response to occupational transition. Data from the 1975 Scottish Mobility Study are used to explore this idea for the period since the First World War. Finally, the idea of labour markets and their segmentation can be used to explicate certain assumptions about mobility processes, and in turn mobility rates are proposed as possible means of identifying labour market boundaries.

Each of the two basic theoretical perspectives provides the necessary framework in which to explain the occupational transition effect. Their significance for the present study is that they offer a series of conceptual reference points so that mobility can be attached to other sociological work in addition to its conventional siting in stratification theory. In so

far as the study attempts new theoretical insights, it is in establishing
such connections. Thus the mobility analysis draws on ideas from the
sociology of labour processes and in turn provides new ways of
examining models of employment which have not previously been
expressed in mobility terms. However, quite deliberately, this book
discusses a range of connections rather than concentrating in detail on
any one, although some ideas like sectoral shift of industries and the
operation of labour markets receive more attention than others. In
borrowing eclectically from both main streams of sociological analysis,
the intention is to offer readers with different theoretical stances a
variety of connections from which they can select those elements which
best fit their own perspective.

However, one consequence of advancing an occupational perspective
on mobility is that some cherished beliefs about class in British society
are brought into question. Chapter 6, for example, is a critique of some
of Glass's findings in the classic *Social Mobility in Britain*. It is argued
that this key work, which has been the basis for so much theorising on
the class structure and provided for over twenty years the cornerstone of
knowledge about mobility, is not so much out of date as inaccurate in its
statement on rates of mobility. Both occupational transition and class
differentials in fertility are used to show that Glass seems to have
underestimated the amount of mobility, as well as pointing us away
from historical effects.

This leaves a substantial gap in our knowledge which is only partially
filled by the recent Oxford survey of England and Wales. The main
account of this research, however, being mainly concerned with
discussions of class, tends to emphasise those aspects of the findings
which emphasise the lack of openness in opportunity in British society.
In order both to fill the vacuum created by these critiques, and to
illustrate how an occupational mobility perspective would operate,
Chapter 7 presents some empirical results (although fuller details are to
be found in Payne, 1986).

Mobility research mainly deals only with men, and it has become conventional (e.g. see Letters to the Editor, *The Times*, 14, 22 and 24 January,
1980), to dismiss mobility research as useless. Although the omission of
women is a serious defect, it does not totally invalidate knowledge
gained about males. A fuller discussion of this problem can be found in
Payne *et al.* (1983a) and some data on female mobility in Scotland in
Payne *et al.* (1980). Because the present account deals with male social
mobility, the use of masculine forms (he, his) throughout is a correct
usage.

In part, this presentation represents a revision of earlier assumptions about rates of mobility by drawing attention to the extent of fluidity in contemporary Britain. The intention is not to argue that British society has an open class structure, but rather that occupational processes result in considerable movements between occupational groupings. Only when this is recognised, is it possible to come to terms with what this means for social class. Thus the discussion emphasises absolute mobility and the present membership of occupational groupings, rather than comparing the disproportionate chances of people from different origins in achieving desirable jobs. A historical account of movements into first jobs is presented, which shows considerable variation in rates of upward mobility, which can in part be related to the occupational opportunity of the particular period that is being reviewed. One important result of this is the discovery of a *decline* in social mobility in the last two decades, which is related to particular patterns of sectoral shift. This perhaps surprising result is obtained only by paying full attention to both the differences between industrial sectors and the detail of historical events.

This book therefore represents a step towards a new perspective. It is not a completed statement, not least because it would be necessary to present a considerable amount of empirical data to develop a number of the propositions that are derived in the course of the exposition. Nor can the present account be complete, because of many of the limitations of both class theory and the study of occupations: for example, the current levels of unemployment, the major question of gender, and the operation of the informal economy are factors which have yet to be fully studied or theorised. If there are limitations to the study of occupations and social class, then in turn mobility analysis inherits these limitations. Nonetheless, in indicating a possible way forward, the present account may well help to develop a better understanding of these complex and changing areas of contemporary debate.

To Judy and Charlie

1 Perspectives on Mobility

One of the peculiarities of social mobility is the way in which it has developed in virtual isolation from the rest of mainstream sociology. Here we have an area of interest to sociologists for more than half a century, and indeed, a major sub-field of research for thirty years, which is so self-contained that it neither draws on the Founding Fathers nor does much to inform current debates about the kind of society in which we live. It is time that this intellectual quarantine be ended.

The main – one might say almost the only – point of contact between mobility and the rest of sociology has been the study of stratification. It therefore should possible to trace the origins of interest in social mobility to earlier sources, as most of sociology's Founding Fathers had something to say about stratification and changes in group membership. For example, Goldthorpe (1980a) has gone to some lengths to show that Marx was aware of social mobility. However, the early writers were more concerned with class, institutions and the division of labour, than with mobility *per se*. This may be one reason for the discontinuity.

It is nevertheless striking that, as Blau and Duncan (1967) have observed, none of the many nineteenth-century theories of social class and differentiation

> had much influence on the systematic research on social mobility that has been carried out in the last two decades. Indeed, most empirical studies of occupational mobility never refer to these theories. Thus even investigators known to be conversant with and sympathetic to Marx's theory do not make reference to it in their mobility research. (Blau and Duncan, 1967, pp. 2–3)

By the same token, one would search Glass's work in vain for reference to nineteenth-century authors as sources of inspiration. Instead, the reader is told that Sorokin's (1927) book 'is still the only comprehensive study' (Glass, 1954, p. 5), and that only Ginsberg (1929) and Carodog Jones (1934) are listed as 'pioneer studies' (Glass, 1954, p. 79 and also pp. 4 and 13).

This is not to suggest, however, that social mobility sprang into sudden, fully-fledged being in 1927 with Sorokin, completely without ancestry. Early writings in the field have drawn on even earlier contributions. For example, Rogoff (1951) – one of the very few sources which Glass does give – mentions the work of Chessa (1912) on recruitment to the Italian professions (Rogoff, 1951, p. 434), while

1

Sorokin includes Pareto and his disciples Kolabinska (1912) on French elites and Sensini (1913) on Italy as sources that provided him with suggestive ideas (Sorokin, 1927, p. 60). But these earlier studies tended to concentrate on recruitment to a single stratum, or to be based on a community study, rather than a national sample covering the whole of society, and it was not until Sorokin's major theoretical statement that the boundaries of the field were laid down.

At the same time, it must be admitted that a great deal of Sorokin's effort to establish social mobility at the heart of sociological concerns bore little fruit. Even when inspired by problems of stratification, mobility research has operated in something of a theoretical vacuum. Little use has been made of classical statements so that the published accounts seem heavily empirical and yet conceptually primitive. It may be fruitless to embark on an extensive historical search for social mobility's intellectual pedigree – and indeed that is something which is not part of the present account – but it is more important to recognise that many social mobility investigators have compartmentalised their research quite separately from their knowledge of sociological theory. Significantly (if we take Britain) it is the *commentators* who have attempted to link Glass's work to ideas about stratification, rather than Glass himself or his main collaborators. Parkin, Westergaard, Giddens, Miliband – and exceptionally Bottomore – are cases in point.

In contrast, this account is an attempt to overcome this separation, and to re-establish connections between mobility, class, and the occupational processes of modern society. It is therefore concerned both with general, macrosociological processes as well as with the nature of stratification in modern Britain. It is not primarily concerned with the consequences for individuals of being socially mobile, such as psychological stress or changes in kinship attachment, as is Richardson (1977). Nor does it make any pretence to express what actors understand by being mobile, to know what the subjective meanings of what the observer calls mobility are for those observed. These are very important questions, but at this stage the first priority is to know more about the canvas on which these more complex issues are displayed. Despite appearances, in fact very little is known about basic patterns of social mobility in Britain: as Chapter 6 argues at some length, what we did think we knew is probably mistaken. Furthermore, the *explanations* of those basic patterns that we draw largely from the 1949 London School of Economics and Political Science study are highly questionable. In particular, an excessive – one might almost say obsessive – concern with education and equality of access have distracted us from the more relevant dimension of occupational mobility and the concomitants of work, careers and changes in employment opportunities. In order to appreciate both this view of mobility and the differences which mark off the present study from its predecessors, the first step is to outline the major contributions to the field of social mobility in the last half century.[1] This will also enable us to see both the potential richness of connections between mobility and general sociology, and the way in which these have yet to be exploited.

SOROKIN'S SOCIAL MOBILITY

Sorokin provides a link between the 'pre-history' and 'history' of social mobility. His work has the character of nineteenth-century writing, ranging from Rome and Athens through medieval England to the contemporary US business elite and back, in an attempt to develop a sociology of industrial society on a grand scale. But it is also the first systematic and comprehensive account of mobility, and despite the limitations of the data available to him at the time, his work is remarkably close to later research findings.

Starting from the notion of a multidimensional 'social space', he proposes

> to reduce the plurality of the dimensions into two principal classes, provided that each is to be subdivided into several sub-classes. These two principal classes may be styled the vertical and the horizontal dimension, dimensions of the social universe. (Sorokin, 1927, p. 7)

The vertical dimension is subdivided into economic (i.e. wealth), political, and occupational components; specific 'channels' are identified – the army, marriage, professional associations, political alliances, and wealth; and different types of society are compared in terms of their flows of vertical mobility, both in 'velocity' and 'volume', through these channels (see particularly pp. 133–80). Sorokin also discusses the role of the family, education, and the employing organisations as mechanisms of selection, or 'sieves' which permit the upward passage of some and deny it to others. At times he seems to adopt an optimistic quasi-functionalist view that the best people get into the best jobs:

> many societies have existed for a long time and this very fact means that their mechnism of social testing, selection, and distributing their

members has not been wholly bad and has performed its function in a more or less satisfactory way. (1927, p. 182: see also pp. 190 and 202).

In other parts of his writing, he recognises that children are dissimilar from their parents, and therefore it is a necessary condition of an efficient society to have 'an equality in the starting point of children and an equality of chance . . . The second fundamental condition is the adequacy of the testing institutions and methods' (1927, p. 530).

More specifically, Sorokin proposes several features of mobility in modern society (pp. 435–9 and pp. 455–6):

1. there is a high level of dispersion of offspring to different occupational groups from those of their fathers
2. all occupational groups consist of members with heterogeneous origins
3. the difference between occupational groups as separate entities is 'blurred'
4. there is, nonetheless, still a high level of occupational inheritance
5. similar occupational groups (ie those adjacent in the occupational hierarchy) are more likely to exchange members
6. mobility is therefore more likely to be 'short-range' than across the whole of the hierarchy
7. the 'middle' of the hierarchy is likely to be more stable than the extremes.

With the possible exception of the last, all of these propositions have since received considerable attention from researchers, and been shown to be generally correct.

Similarly, Sorokin's work on the consequences of mobility in one dimension for behaviour in another has also inspired later sociologists, although here the emphasis has shifted. Sorokin writes about psychological dislocation, mental illness, suicide and moral disintegration (in a Durkheimian sense) among the mobile as consequences of isolation from intimate friendships and close kinship ties requiring many years to establish (pp. 508–27). Although a few writers have speculated along these lines (e.g. Lipset and Bendix, 1959, pp. 285; Stacey, 1967) a more fruitful line of inquiry has been to examine the extent to which mobility does reduce kinship interaction or community involvement: later sociologists have generally been less alarmist (for example see Litwak, 1960a, and 1960b; Adams, 1968; Bell, 1968; Richardson, 1977; Goldthorpe, 1980a).

At this distance, the sense of anxiety about mobility in modern society is one of the things that strikes the contemporary reader. In talking about horizontal mobility, Sorokin likens modern society to

> a mad 'merry-go-round' in which men, objects and values incessantly move with a mad rapidity, shift, turn round, clash, struggle, appear, disappear, diffuse, without a moment of rest and stability. Compared with immobile societies in all these respects they offer a contrast to them no less striking than that of boiling water or a waterfall to a quiet pond or lake. (Sorokin, 1927, pp. 394)

This somewhat overdramatic style may have been a contributory factor to the 'distortion' of Sorokin's conception of social mobility by later sociologists. As was noted above, his mobility was a multidimensional one, including not only several subdivisions of vertical space, but subdivisions of horizontal space as well. Modern mobility research has concentrated almost exclusively on mobility as vertical occupational movements, although as we shall see later in this chapter, this has been treated as if it were social mobility in a more general sense. The present study attempts to rectify this, not by exploring other vertical subdivisions, but by explicitly confronting the occupational dimension.

It also draws on another neglected feature in Sorokin's work, namely the role of historical events (1927, pp. 142 and 466). Contained in his panoramic review of human history is a very simple and sensible point: societies are disrupted by wars, revolutions, famines and other natural disasters. These real events remove the incumbents of occupational strata (as in the Russian Revolution), kill off competitors (as in the First World War), or speed up circulation (as in periods of economic boom). The process of mobility is bedded in a concrete time and place, and yet modern analysts have almost nothing to say about world wars, depressions, or even technological change. Their world is a rarified place of statistical relationships with little reference to the twentieth century and its complex changes. Had Sorokin had better data available to him, he might have been able to demonstrate his point to greater effect.

Even nearly twenty years later, when with the LSE study of Britain in 1949 this kind of evidence did become available, subsequent writers failed to take up the question of historical settings. The 1949 study was historical in the sense that it was concerned with the effects of the 1944 Education Act, but it went little beyond that. There are no index entries for 'war' or 'unemployment', and only four for the Depression – all in Jean Floud's chapter on the educational experiences of adults. In this, and in many other respects, *Social Mobility in Britain* typifies the next generation of mobility studies.

SOCIAL MOBILITY IN BRITAIN

Of the three major contributions which have been identified at the start of this chapter, the work of David Glass and the LSE team is the most important. It not only provided a conceptual and technical orientation for later research but also produced empirical evidence about mobility that was taken up by other sociologists for the next twenty years. The fact that it was a study of Britain of course makes it all the more relevant for the present project.

The major publication arising from their work, *Social Mobility in Britain* (Glass, 1954) is a collection of cognate chapters ranging over education, marriage, and mobility, technical problems of statistical analysis, and reports of work on voluntary associations, the professions, and subjective class ratings carried out separately from the main national sample. Of these it is the sections dealing with social mobility *per se* which are most relevant, together with the introductory explanations of why the researchers tackled their tasks in a particular way. Glass gives priority of place in his opening remarks to two themes, an interest in 'the formation and structure of the "middle classes"', and in the consequences of the passing of the 1944 Education Act 'which, so far as social stratification is concerned, is probably the most important measure of the last half-century' (1954, pp. 3 and 4).

Glass's interest in the middle classes, by which he seems to mean mainly the professions and the higher civil service (e.g. see pp. 4–5), led him to look at the wider picture as a first step:

> Self-recruitment in the professions and the higher Civil Service would have little meaning unless compared with self-recruitment in other occupational groups. Indeed, it was clear that the study of particular groups needed, as background, a *general* investigation of social status and social mobility in Britain. (1954, pp. 4–5)

It would not be unfair to say that the British working-class features in the LSE research more as a by-product than as a main focus of the analysis.

Because of this orientation, there is paradoxically not a great deal of the section dealing with the main investigation in *Social Mobility in Britain* which is about class differences (except in relation to educational access). Although extensive data are presented in the various mobility tables, there is little commentary on, or use of, them to discuss class boundaries, class consciousness and integration, or the rigidity of the class structure as a whole. These were issues taken up later by writers who saw the potential of Glass's evidence for class analysis. What little original discussion there was dealt mainly with the upper occupational strata, rather than the lower.

In the same way, the team's interest in educational reform was to see what effect it might have upon the existing middle classes and 'its role in the formation of new elites' (Glass, 1954, p. 4). The 1944 Act would reduce the effect of family background on the type of secondary education received, so that 'social mobility will increase, and probably increase greatly' (1954, p. 24).

This would be a desirable result for two reasons. First it would increase economic and social efficiency,

> since with a fluid social structure there is more likelihood that positions requiring high ability will in fact be held by individuals who possess high ability . . . secondly, from the point of view of the individual . . . there may, as a consequence, be less feeling of personal frustration and a greater possibility of social harmony (1954, pp. 24–5).

Not surprisingly, later writers (for example Kreckel, 1973 and Goldthorpe, 1980a, pp. 21–3) have commented adversely on this rather narrow conception of what is problematic about social mobility. There is no concern with equality of condition, only equality of access. The harsh realities (according to Glass's own data) of a relatively closed class system, the privileges of the middle class and the deprivations of the working class, feature little in the commentary. The orientation is liberal social democrat or 'Fabian'; the product is 'rather bloodless, rather statistical', to use Strauss's phrase about social mobility in general (Strauss, 1971, p. 2).

Goldthorpe has recently argued slightly more generously that Glass was *also* concerned with equality of condition in that he opposed private education and wished to avoid meritocratic selection leading to a new, more legitimate but still powerful elite. This may be true as a judgement of Glass as a man, but whereas Goldthorpe himself produces several quotations from Glass which show the latter as a Fabian meritocrat, he produces only a single one to substantiate his assertion that Glass was also a socialist seeking major social change – and that quotation, read in context, is extremely ambiguous, for the 'other paths to social prestige' need not refer to any humanistic or socialist values, but are discussed in the same conflict-reducing framework that was noted above (see Goldthorpe, 1980a, pp. 23, and Glass, 1954, pp. 26–7).

While one sympathises with Glass in the sense that he was writing soon after the 1944 Act in a period when Labour Party hopes were still high, and that his general investigation of social mobility was an important step forward for its time, this should not blind us to the limitations of his position. In the light of the Scottish data, for example, Glass's concern with education as a reforming factor is to say the least, questionable (Payne *et al.*, 1979) and the emphasis on the middle class means that other issues received less attention. In particular, as this chapter goes on to argue, the occupational structure itself was so neglected as to distort not only the LSE study, but also to influence later writers (among them, members of the International Sociological Association Social Stratification and Social Mobility Group which first met in 1951) so that the *occupational* dimension of mobility remained virtually unexplored for the next twenty years.

Most important of all, the present author is extremely sceptical about the core findings on mobility rates in the LSE study. This is such a fundamental question to raise, as well as being based on a technical argument, that it deserves a chapter to itself. Glass's results are therefore not discussed at this point, but in Chapter 6.

Nonetheless, it must be acknowledged that Glass's work has been absolutely central to the mobility field. In this country it effectively put an end to further mobility research for a generation, because after 1954 we 'knew' about mobility and could use what was known as the basis for writing on stratification. Sociologists like Parkin and Westergaard (and others, see Chapter 6) felt no need to get involved in new data-collection exercises, when patterns of mobility had been so clearly demonstrated. The influence of Glass was, then, in terms of his *results* as far as Britain was concerned, whereas internationally it was the *techniques and the novelty* of the research itself which helped to inspire comparable national studies throughout most of Europe, the USA, and eventually in Japan, Australia, and much of the Third World. It was one of the key inspirations of the third main contribution to the development of social mobility, that of Blau and Duncan.

THE AMERICAN OCCUPATIONAL STRUCTURE

Blau and Duncan's work was by no means the first on social mobility in America, (see for instance Sjoberg (1951); Rogoff (1951); Hollingshead (1952); Chinoy (1955); Lenski (1958); and Lipset and Bendix (1964)) but like the LSE study in its time, it was more comprehensive, technically more sophisticated, and conceptually more developed than previous efforts.

Using a sample of 20,700 respondents representing about 45 million men 20 to 64 years old in the civilian, non-institutionalised population, they analysed not only occupational mobility but also the relationship between mobility and migration, ethnicity, kinship, and fertility patterns. In particular they attempted to demonstrate how family background factors (parental education and employment) operated on and through the respondent's own schooling, and first job, to produce the respondent's current socio-economic status. This involved the use of path analysis, a technique which dominated US mobility research for the next decade. In essence, path analysis uses multiple regression techniques to parcel out effects between variables in a simple model that is chronologically structured. Once the model is established, it can be used to make causal statements about how changes in the level of one variable bring about changes in the dependent variable. Again, the Blau and Duncan model can be elaborated from its original quintet of variables by adding more variables, which improves its effectiveness.[2]

Despite its initial attractiveness, path analysis has not been much adopted by what we might call the 'European sociological tradition'. In part, this is due to a number of important technical features of path analysis: for example, there are limitations on the comparison between one survey and another; the variables are assumed to be normally distributed; the excluded variables (which by definition, there must be in a simple model) reduce the explanatory power of the model and must be treated as causally irrelevant, and so on. An excellent critique of path analysis in mobility research is to be found in Crowder (1974). However, the lack of popularity of path analysis is also due to its association with the conceptual framework in which Blau and Duncan operated.

Blau and Duncan regard social mobility primarily as a process of status attainment, which in industrial society is dominated by universalistic values. Ascriptive factors like family background must play an increasingly small part in deciding occupational fates, because achievement factors such as educational qualifications and work performance are necessarily more important when it comes to filling posts that require technical skill, where the efficient discharge of work tasks is essential to the working of a technological society. What Blau and Duncan call the 'universalistic system' (1967, p. 430) produces technological progress, high standards of living, greater equality of opportunity, reduced kinship ties, higher rates of migration, differential fertility, 'stable democracy', and high rates of occupational mobility (1967, pp. 430–31).

It is possible to object to this view in two ways. First, one could make the point by point objections, such as the continued existence of ethnic and sexual discrimination, i.e. discrimination on ascriptive characteristics, which is not explained by such a model. Second, one can object that the whole orientation of the approach is misplaced: the role of property and power are completely omitted from consideration, and the fate of identifiable classes or strata is lost under the associated assumption that under universalism, 'the occupational structure is more or less continuously graded in regard to status rather than being a set of discrete status classes' (Blau and Duncan, 1967, p. 124). In other words, one can approach stratification not as the outcome of a value system, but rather as the social product of a particular set of class relations arising from the dominant mode of production under modern capitalism. In one view, the value system is the paramount consideration, in the other, it is the relations of production. Although the present study adopts the latter view, it is worth noting that Blau and Duncan still manage to compare the positions of working and middle classes, and that their framework does not exclude family background or differential access to education as relevant objects of study.

OTHER THEMES IN MOBILITY RESEARCH

Sorokin, Glass, and Blau and Duncan were key influences on mobility research. They all stimulated new interest in mobility, but whereas Sorokin had opened up a broad conception of the phenomenon, the others effectively closed it down. To be fair, they did acknowledge these wider issues, but the emphasis in their publications lay elsewhere. Of course, not all of their contemporaries did exactly the same research and while one may wish to stress the a-theoretical nature of mobility research, it was not totally so. Not least among other themes to receive attention was comparison of mobility rates between different societies.

We have already commented on the effect that Glass's work, via the ISA, had on stimulating national studies. Given the centrality of the structural questions to which he addressed himself, other sociologists in different countries naturally wished to examine their own societies to see if patterns of mobility were similar to those Glass had reported for England and Wales. This in turn provided the basis for comparison between societies, most notably those of Lipset and Bendix (1959) and Miller (1960). The variety of occupational categorisation schemes used made this a difficult task and one of doubtful value: Miller's discussion of elites, for example, defines an elite as consisting variously of anything from 0.9 per cent to over 15 per cent of the population, while Lipset and Bendix's conclusion that 'the overall pattern of social mobility appears to be much the same in the industrial societies of various Western Countries' (1964, p. 13) is based only on movements across the manual/non-manual line.[3]

These international comparisons reflect an interest in the openness of class boundaries in different societies, most notably possible differences between US and the European societies, which has origins in early ideological statements about the American way of life, and in sociology, in the work of Sombart (1906) and Sorokin (1927). This in turn is related to the problem of social and political order, which is a much more important feature of, say, Lipset and Bendix's work, than Glass or Blau and Duncan.

One of the first concerns which Lipset and Bendix discussed in *Social Mobility in Industrial Society* is the problem facing any ruling class: to exclude potential incomers from the lower ranks, or to admit them? Which is the more threatening to the continuance of their power? *The* issue in the complex area of mobility and class structure becomes access to the elite, rather than the position of the middle classes, or the working class, while the notion of mobility as inherently desirable is questioned. Moving away from a stable social group sets up pressures on the individual and may weaken the stability of the system as a whole. As Goldthorpe has recently observed in a discussion of interest and ideology in mobility research,

> the theme recurs that an unremitting emphasis on universalistic values may lead ultimately to socially disruptive rather than to socially integrative effects. (Goldthorpe 1980a, p. 19)

Successive generations of American sociologists have drawn on this tradition. The size and regional variation of the USA has proved a fertile site, while the greater technical sophistication of US methodology has both prompted more interest in what is a heavily statistical field, and also stimulated new techniques of analysis. Following Blau and Duncan, new forms of the basic path model were proposed (for example, see Sewell *et al.*, 1969) and more recently Hauser *et al.* (1975a and b) have introduced log-linear modelling techniques to disaggregate structural effects. There have been two kinds of reaction against these developments. The first criticism is that the theoretical orientation attaches too great an importance to mobility as against other aspects of the class structure, and tends to be supportive of a false notion of the

USA as an open society (e.g. Osipov, 1969; Bertaux, 1971; Kreckel, 1973). The second criticism is that the technical elaboration of the analysis has distorted the kinds of questions being tackled and that many of the statistical techniques are inappropriate for the uses to which they have been put (Crowder, 1974; Noble, 1981).

Although social mobility research in Europe has also become more technically sophisticated, it has not done so to the extent of the US work. Interest in the last few years has turned to alternative perspectives: Müller (1977) for example has argued that real historical events (like the rise of the Nazis in Germany, and the Second World War) must feature in an explanation of mobility, while an interest in the complexity of individual mobility records has led some studies to examine complete occupational histories (as in the Irish Mobility Study). Despite these divergent approaches, there is a strong undercurrent of interest in class (see Girod, 1974), which marks off almost all the European work from that in the USA.

MOBILITY AND CLASS

This is clearly exemplified by the centrality of class in publications resulting from the Nuffield Study of Social Mobility in England and Wales. Heath's opening sentence in *Social Mobility* poses the question, 'How are men to be recruited to positions of power and privilege?', while he takes as the first 'landmark' in the development of answers to this question to be 'Karl Marx and class formation' (Heath, 1981, pp. 11 and 13). Similarly Goldthorpe's main report on the Nuffield Study is entitled *Social Mobility and Class Structure in Modern Britain*, starts with a chapter dealing largely with Marx on class, and uses the term 'class mobility' in five of its eight other chapter headings (Goldthorpe, 1980a; see also p. 287).

Heath and Goldthorpe are only two of the more recent writers to see class and mobility as essentially related. A number of different positions go to make up this dominant approach, including accounts of particular classes as well as comparative analysis of societies. In this approach, mobility is a measure of rigidity of the stratified order over time: high rates of mobility suggest a system in which, despite whatever inequalities may exist at any one time, more people (or rather their families) have access to the more desirable statuses in the long term. Conversely, low levels of mobility indicate a highly stratified, caste-like, order in which inequalities apply to successive generations. US sociologists in the 1950s and early 1960s, such as Bendix and Lipset, were particularly keen to compare societies for their degrees of openness or closure in this way. More recently Goldthorpe's collaboration with several European sociologists (e.g. Erikson *et al*. 1979 and 1981) demonstrates a renewal of interest in this approach.

A second connection between class and mobility comes in the use of mobility rates to identify the boundaries of classes. Those statuses which readily exchange members can be thought of as having more in common than those between which exchange is limited. An examination of the 'natural breaks' in the mobility flows reveals the basic class structure, while changes over time in such breaks indicate changes in the shape of society, and the relative success or failure of groups in narrowing or maintaining the gaps between the classes. Recent examples of this approach can be found in the work of Parkin, Westergaard and Resler, and the Marxist debate over the class position of 'the new middle classes'.

A third use of mobility in stratification theory is as an explanation of class consciousness (or more precisely, lack of it). If there is considerable movement between classes, then the present members of any class are more likely to have been born and socialised in some other class. That is to say, they will bring with them values and experiences appropriate to a different way of life, which will prevent them from belonging as completely and unquestioningly to their new class as those who have been born into, and lived all their lives in, that class. Indeed, their imported values may 'infect' the host population leading to a 'mongrelisation' of class values. In this way (following Sorokin) there is less chance of a distinctive class consciousness emerging, or for in-comers to acquire it should one begin to develop. In turn, there is less prospect of collective class action. Albeit expressed in less overtly Marxist terms, Giddens and writers on the new managerial class like Galbraith and Crosland have adopted this argument.

A final example of the close conjunction between stratification and social mobility is political stability. Two perspectives can be differentiated here: on the one hand, mobility is seen as a safety valve used to bleed off working-class pressure for change, by allowing the most able to pass into the ranks of the middle class, so leaving the working class without effective leadership. In this view, mobility appears as a mechanism of control, which serves to perpetuate the capitalist order. As Marx observes: 'The more a ruling class is able to assimilate the most prominent men of the ruled class the more solid and dangerous is its rule' (Marx 1959a, p. 706).

The alternative view stresses the pacification effect on the unsuccessful (or immobile) of believing either that the able really do succeed, or that their own lack of success does not preclude their children from being mobile. Here the emphasis is more on legitimation, rather than control, but in both mobility is used to explain the continued survival of an inequitable and otherwise insupportable system (e.g. the writings of Michels and Sombart).

DEVELOPING A NEW MOBILITY PERSPECTIVE

In the preceding discussion, the question of stratification has been ever-present, but two broad themes emerge. First, in the work of the earlier writers, connections were made to a range of sociological issues. Sorokin sees mobility as multi-dimensional, Glass deals with educational reforms, Blau and Duncan identify universalism as a new feature of modern society, and Bendix and Lipset adopt a comparative political standpoint. Their various contributions are open to criticism, but they do on the whole seek to situate mobility in a wide sociological context. What is remarkable is the way in which their concerns with wider issues failed to be taken up by mobility researchers, who instead became increasingly more specialised.

In as far as mobility research can be said to have a theoretical concern, it is stratification that has driven out the other wider issues. Work on mobility particularly in Europe has been highly focused on class, and so without the driving force of sociology's central interest in stratification and social order, mobility would not have assumed its current place in the sociological lexicon. However, the very strength of the connection between mobility and stratification has, paradoxically, narrowed our awareness of mobility and the way it relates to other sociological problems.

This has resulted in a failure to realise the potential of mobility analysis to contribute to a wide range of sociological debate. It has also hampered the development of a proper understanding of the relationship between class and mobility itself. Central to this is the way in which mobility researchers have on the whole neglected the social context in which mobility occurs and the way in which *class mobility* is in fact based in *occupational mobility*. We cannot account for class mobility unless we first examine the occupational dimension.

An occupational approach grounds mobility firmly in the local economic, social and historical conditions of the society in which it occurs. Since mobility operationally constitutes a comparison of two occupational statuses (the father's and the son's) an explanation of mobility involves an explanation of how individuals come to be given jobs. This in turn raises questions about the industrial and occupational structure, about labour markets, about job choice and qualifications, about labour migration: that is, about the various processes by which workers enter a system of employment which has an objective reality pre- and post-existing the individual, and which constrains his or her freedom of action.

The comparatively simple idea of looking at local conditions, and in particular of taking the idea of *occupational* mobility seriously, is in fact a major departure from earlier work like the Nuffield Study, or Glass. It represents a marked shift in emphasis for mobility research away from conventional class theory and towards other aspects of sociology, notably the sociology of work and the labour requirements of modern societies. In that sense, although this study does relate to more recent work, it looks back more to Sorokin than to much of the other writing discussed.

2 Mobility, Occupations and Class

In looking at work and mobility we may begin by asking mundane questions about work processes in life cycles. How do men obtain employment, or lose it; what are the requirements for promotion, why do men change jobs, and so on? These kinds of questions mean that we take the metaphor of occupational mobility seriously, and narrow down our focus from the grand horizon of stratification theory to the more commonplace world of work. This does not imply that we are concerned solely with work tasks, or that we are abandoning our earlier statement that occupation cannot be isolated from other aspects of stratification. Rather, we are recognising that our view of stratification, if based on occupation, is conditioned by the processes which themselves condition occupations. The other side of this proposed concentration on occupation operates in the reverse direction; we can expand our interest by asking wider, historical questions, such as how do social changes generate new patterns of occupations, patterns which in turn account for observed mobility? In other words, we need to consider theories of the evolution of advanced industrial society, or the emergence of modern capitalism, which either directly or indirectly deal with occupational processes.

Both of these elaborations of the more conventional approach to mobility are basically very simple ideas. If mobility is measured by means of occupations, then the commonsense explanation of mobility lies in whatever determines the supply of and access to those occupations. Starting in a concrete way, we can examine the society of our choice much as an economic or social historian would. It is possible to describe changes in the size of the labour force, its gender, its industrial composition, and its work skills: the census will provide a decennial framework for this. Other official sources (such as emigration and unemployment figures), memoires, and company histories may describe how certain older industries declined, while elsewhere other industries based on new technologies developed, so contracting some occupations, and expanding others. Again, major events like the Great Depression and the two world wars must have made some kind of difference to the employment histories of men of working age during them. It may also be possible to analyse the regional or segmented

16

labour markets which make up the national picture. Men are not universal units of labour in a society-wide market: rather, they are restricted by social ties and the friction of space to selling their labour in only one localised segment of the total market at any one time.

Presented in this fashion, the proposed analysis sounds almost pedestrian in its obviousness. But the reader will look in vain for such a treatment in the literature on social mobility in Britain, and will need to search with great diligence to find even partial programmatic statements among European writers (see, for example Bertaux, 1969 and Müller, 1971)[1]. It is true that the main thrust of research into the relationship between education and mobility seeks to locate mobility in a framework of legislation, institutional practice and educational reform (Little and Westergaard, 1964; Halsey *et al.*, 1980). However, such analyses have concentrated on class differentials in access, and there is an inadequate recognition of occupational change and the full range of historical factors involved.

And yet the basis for a sociographic approach can be found in the works of Sorokin and Glass, who both talk about historical and demographic changes. Indeed, the latter initiated one of the key technical debates in measuring mobility; the attempt to eliminate 'the effect of the marginals'. It was early seen that in a mobility table, the size of the origin categories, relative to the destination categories, imposed arithmetic limits on the amount and kind of mobility that could take place. Numerous indices were proposed to control for this effect, so that the remaining 'true' mobility could be estimated for comparison with other societies or previous eras. It has been conventional to distinguish in this way between fathers' and sons' occupational distributions, and 'pure' mobility.

While such an analytical distinction may be of interest, it is something of a false dichotomy. The occupational distributions of a given era in a given society are not inconveniences which obscure mobility rates, but rather the specific framework in which mobility takes place. They are at the centre of the problem to be explored, not something of relative unimportance to be controlled for by deft statistical manipulation or left uninvestigated.

The debate about 'structural' and 'exchange' mobility is as close as mainstream mobility analysis has come to tackling the difference between social and occupational mobility. In Europe, researchers have on the whole used occupations as if they are non-problematic representations of social classes. This is not, of course, a problem unique to mobility research nor can it be made to disappear by concentrating on the occupational dimension. On the contrary, it becomes all the more important to be precise about how we shall use terms like occupation, class and mobility, if only because we are using the first as a means of understanding the other two concepts.

OCCUPATIONS AND SOCIAL MOBILITY

When modern sociologists have talked about social mobility, they have normally concentrated on intergenerational (and to a lesser extent, intragenerational) occupational mobility among men. In practical terms, this has generally meant comparing a son's job with that of his father. The son's job may be his first job, or his job after ten years of work, or three years ago, or more commonly, his job at the time of interview. These are the four 'job points' examined in both the Oxford study of England and Wales in 1972, and the Aberdeen study of 1975. Some more recent European studies have concentrated on parts of a career (Müller, 1977), while others, including the Irish Mobility Study, have collected whole life employment histories.

The father's job has been taken as his present or last job (Glass, 1954) or his job at some stage in the adolescence of the son, usually dependent on the school-leaving age of a particular country during a particular period. In Britain, the age of fourteen has been chosen in recent studies. The movement of a son between the two social statuses defined by his own adult membership of one occupational group, and his previous indirect membership, by virtue of his juvenile family position, of his father's occupational group, is occupational mobility. Intragenerational mobility refers to movements during one man's lifetime between any two job points that he has occupied.

In most writing about mobility, the terms 'social mobility' and 'occupational mobility' are used synonymously, a practice which will be followed here in the interests of variety and familiarity. However, it is important to recognise at the very outset that strictly speaking mobility is measured in an occupational dimension. The mainstream European tradition has used occupation in a direct way, with similar jobs grouped together in broad categories or 'classes' (again, there is a conventional and imprecise use of the word class for any occupational grouping). The Americans have preferred to measure mobility between socio-economic statuses, based indirectly on job, and expressing some weighting for income, education and prestige ranking. However, it is no coincidence that writings about 'social' and 'occupational' mobility between 'classes' have used these imprecise terms interchangeably. Certainly in Europe, few sociologists have been interested in mobility *per se*, or even as an aspect of *occupational* processes. Far more important has been a concern with social stratification, in which occupation is taken as a convenient indicator of class membership, and occupational movement stands for movement between classes or statuses.

Of course, it must be said that the equation of occupation and social class is a well-established one in British sociology. In the first place, 'social class' is itself a complex social phenomenon. Unless class is defined in some very precise way one immediately becomes enmeshed in the interface with other dimensions of stratification such as status and political power; and even if class is taken in its narrowest sense, that pitfall is never far away. Reid compares the conceptual and practical side of the problem:

> Social class is a multidimensional concept, involving not only the identification of what are partly invisible categories in society but also an understanding of the effects of these on the people involved . . . In British research . . . almost the sole criterion of social class which has been used is occupation. (Reid, 1977, p. 15)

Reid is saying that on the one hand it is not possible to contain the notion of class in a simple economic or market straightjacket, and on the other, that there is a legitimate tradition of using occupations as a pragmatic device in the empirical exploration of class. The latter is generally accepted in Britain by sociologists with widely different persuasions. Runciman has observed that 'Occupations are at once the most obvious and the most effective predictor of differential location within the structure of social inequality' (Runciman, 1966, p. 55), while on the heavily empirical flank, Monk, a former employee of the SSRC Survey Research Unit, notes that 'Occupation has remained the backbone of social grading because no better methods have been found' (Monk, 1970, p. 10).

Occupation has been generally chosen because it provides a simple, universal and relatively unambiguous identity (or rather it did until sociologists woke up to the fact that females, too, need a class identity, but that many of them do not have occupations that carry the same meaning as for men). Occupation carries with it connotations of income, and therefore possible patterns of consumption; levels of skill and educational entry requirements, and therefore life styles; sets of opinions, values and attitudes and therefore political behaviours; collectivities of work-based friendships, and therefore group identity;

social prestige and therefore influence outside of the work setting; even patterns of fertility and mortality are associated with occupational groupings. Since all of these factors are part of the stratified order, and are all in various degrees correlated with occupation, it has been taken as the single and simplest indicator of position within a social hierarchy.

This is to say two things about occupations in previous and in the present work. First, occupation *represents* other aspects of stratification because it is highly *correlated* with them. But second, occupation is inherently *connected* to other aspects of stratification, so that the analytical distinction between occupation and these other features is a heuristic device. In particular, in stressing the centrality of occupations for purposes of examining hierarchy, the *cluster* of connected features remains important, however unstated, despite what might at first sight be a treatment of occupation conceived of narrowly as a set of work tasks.

CONCEPTUALISING OCCUPATIONS AND CLASSES

Indeed, even if one takes a narrow view of occupation as something restricted to the work place, it would be inadequate to regard occupation as a set of technical skill tasks. As Bechhofer's (1969) survey has shown, there is a long-established practice of using occupation to convey a variety of ideas. Two main components have most commonly been emphasised: 'the precise job description, with the focus on the work content; and the position in the industrial hierarchy, with the focus on the internal stratification of industry' (Bechhofer, 1969, p. 99). *Both* of these are important, not least in discussing how occupations can be used to represent classes.

A contrary view can be found in recent Marxist writing, in which the technical division of labour and the social division of labour are kept separate. Here occupation *per se* is less important, and while the technical division of labour is relevant for discussions of how surplus value is extracted, it is the relationship *between* classes that retains theoretical primacy. Thus Abercrombie and Urry (1982) argue that:

> although occupational designations are very often used as a convenient shorthand for class position, they are not theoretically equivalent. Occupation typically refers primarily to sets of job tasks, that is, it refers to positions within the technical division of labour . . . the concept of class refers primarily to the social relations at work, or

positions within the social division of labour ... Occupational designations may actually obscure class position because technical features do not entail social features. (Abercombie and Urry, 1982, p. 109)

At one level, this is a valid observation: the *employed* professional and the *self-employed* professional carry out many of the same technical functions but occupy different class positions. On the other hand, a sharp distinction between 'job task' and social relationships makes it difficult to specify the job tasks of certain people, such as a foreman or manager whose work task is to occupy an authority relationship over others. While technical task may be a starting point for identifying occupational categories, as in census and other classifications of occupations (Bechhofer, 1969, p. 98) the role within the enterprise must be treated as an integral part of occupational identity if a full picture is to be gained.

This position has been built into the classification scheme used in the Scottish Mobility Study. Unlike the scheme used by Goldthorpe (1980a) and Halsey *et al.* (1980), the classification developed for the Scottish study made explicit and rigorous use of the 'employment status' (manager, foreman, employee, etc.) which was part of the original grading exercise in the preliminaries for devising the Hope–Goldthorpe scale. Thus each 'occupational class' so defined reflects a similarity of task *and* authority, and possibly also of status as perceived by the respondents who graded them, among its component occupations. This is not to say that occupations will be treated as identical to class, but that the distinction between the two in some respects has been reduced.

Indeed, the 'occupational class' as used in this study is very reminiscent of Lockwood's statement of 'class situation'. People in a common occupational class share similar levels of skills in order to carry out the technical tasks of their jobs. Their skill level defines to a large degree their market situation, i.e., their source of income and its size, their job security and mobility chances. Their common employment position expresses comparable sets of social relationship at work, derived from similar positions in the division of labour; that is to say, a common work situation. And the ranking of the occupations, whatever the origin intentions of Hope and Goldthorpe, probably reflect common positions in the status hierarchy, or a shared status situation.[2]

One other of the key dimensions used in identifying occupations with classes, property, was given a relatively low priority in the Scottish Mobility Study occupational classes, for two reasons. First, the number of people in certain proprietorial positions in any national study sample is very small; the category of substantial proprietor has been for empirical purposes merged with that of managers. Very small-scale businessmen (self-employed non-professional workers without employees) are treated as part of the same group as foremen and supervisors. This reflects their actual grading scores and recognises that to become a foreman, or 'set up on one's own' is a common, if not always realistic, occupational goal for many manual workers. However, the idea of large property (as against petty property) differentiating a capitalist class from the ordinary men in the sample is retained as an important element, even if it is not manifest in the main occupational class scheme. Similarly, the petty bourgeois are not identified as a separate class, but could be separated out if required. The concept of skill as 'property', and the ownership and control debate, are discussed in the course of the following chapters. The occupational classes are therefore more 'occupational' than 'classes', in that they do not take into account property or result directly through theorising from modes of production.

This does not mean that mobility is conceived as existing simply in a concrete dimension of individuals on the move. Both occupations and classes can be thought of as positions or as people. In mobility research this is central, because people are seen as leaving one position and moving to another. The position, and the composite structure of all positions, is separate from the person moving. This accords with everyday life: a job is created, advertised, and filled. The new incumbent works in the job for a while and then leaves for another job. The post is then refilled by someone else. Employment is dependent on the pre-existence of a position.

It is therefore possible to talk about occupations at both levels. In a mobility study one talks about, say, the patterns of recruitment to the professions and empirically represents the professions as places by examining those people in the sample who reported that they worked as professionals. In principle at least one could add to this some measure of employment vacancies and unemployed professionals, in order to have a fuller account of opportunity. This would deal more directly, albeit still empirically, with positions, while the simple approach deals with individuals.

The distinction is sometimes hard to sustain, but it can play an important part, as in the work of Stewart *et al.* (1980) on clerks and clerical employment. They argue that the position of clerical worker is filled almost exclusively by young men on their way up to managerial positions and old men who are former manual workers. It is not a position containing persons who have worked or intend to work for long periods as clerks. Thus although at any one time clerks may have similar work tasks and hierarchical positions, it makes little sense to talk of them occupying a common position because their origins and destinations are so diverse. While their point that persons carry with them 'social baggage' from, or ready for, another occupational or class position is a strong one, their rejection of clerical work as a useful category is dependent on its unique mobility characteristics. Other occupational categories are more useful, if only because their incumbents remain in them for longer periods.

We may contrast this view of persons and places with that of Poulantzas, who argues that even if 'the bourgeoisie would take all the places of workers and vice versa, nothing fundamental about capitalism would be changed since the places of bourgeoisie and proletariat would still be there' (Poulantzas, 1975, p. 33). While recognising Poulantzas' wish to attach importance to capitalist relations, he is not correct in claiming that people ('social agents' in his form) are irrelevant to class analysis. If people are mobile, their 'social baggage' is not lost in transit, even if much of it is no longer used on arrival. A bourgeois who was formerly a member of the proletariat is not the same as someone who has lived all his life in the bourgeoisie. It is this fact that makes analysis of class such a difficult empirical problem, and which acts in real life to reduce and confuse class differences.

Class is also a difficult problem because it is a changing one. Like both the structure of occupations and rates of mobility, social class changes as societies develop historically. In taking the metaphor of occupational mobility seriously, the new question is no longer what do changing rates of mobility tell us about the evolving class structure, but rather what does a study of mobility tell us about the evolution and character of the particular type of society which has existed in this country during this century? Of course, this still remains partly a matter of stratification. If 'the particular type of society' is defined as advanced capitalism, then class is going to remain one of the central issues. Even writers who have adopted one of the rival definitions of contemporary society (as 'advanced industrial' or 'post industrial' society) do not ignore the form which stratification takes, even if their conclusions are quite different from those of the Marxists. However, the emphasis and ordering of problems will not be the same, if only because there must be a more explicit reference to ideas about the nature of a society which is based on an advanced technology, and specifically about occupational change.

OCCUPATIONS AND OCCUPATIONAL MOBILITY

To what extent can changes in the occupational structure be said to *explain* patterns of mobility? By definition, an expansion or a contraction of an occupational group changes the overall flow of recruitment to (and from) that group. Such a change manifests itself as an arithmetic relationship in a mobility table; in both real and analytical terms, the change in the recruitment is *caused* by the change in the occupational structure. It does not, however, explain the details of the new recruitment. The new recruits to an expanded occupation may come more from other groups in the upper part of the hierarchy, or from the same groups, or from lower groups – or the new posts may be shared out in exactly the same proportions as before.

Although this last possibility seems unlikely at first sight, it is not completely implausible. *If one assumes for the moment that the mechanisms of selection (in Sorokin's sense) do not change*, then the allocation of people to the new posts within an expanding occupation will favour (and discriminate against) exactly the same kinds of people as before. Until the point is reached where *all* of these potentially eligible people have been allocated, and there are still 'vacancies', the incomers will just be 'more of the same'. After all, past recruits have come from diverse backgrounds, so that it is unlikely that the criteria for selection are so precise as to restrict entry to a very small sub-set of the population which can be exhausted before the expansion has been filled up.

We can qualify this statement to take account of what is generally known about occupational change, i.e. that it is the non-manual occupations that are growing in both absolute and relative terms. This growth is of two kinds, the expansion in size of existing occupations, and the creation of completely new occupations. In new occupations there are at first no formal rules of entry, no union or professional association to limit access. New recruits are people from other very similar occupations who drift across into a new specialism. The new occupation attracts members much like its closest ancestors even if its formal qualifications are not established. This in turn tends to make its later history of selection like those other occupations, at least in terms of the origins of its recruits.

Being in the upper part of the occupational hierarchy means that increased recruitment on the previous pattern has two effects. It offers more non-manual careers to the sons of non-manual fathers, so increasing immobility and cutting downward mobility. At the same time it offers more non-manual careers to the sons of manual fathers, so reducing immobility and increasing upward mobility. The joint effect is to reduce downward mobility, and to produce some kind of balanced effect on immobility and upward mobility, depending on the precise recruitment pattern reproduced. Because the original pattern of recruitment is one that selects from diverse origins, there is no automatic outcome beyond this. It would be just as wrong to assume that non-manual sons will benefit most, so increasing immobility, as to assume that manual sons will benefit most, so increasing upward mobility.

Again we have built into this model the further assumption that recruitment is from diverse origins, which it is (as we shall see on page 123). However, there is an additional broad patterning to the relationship between origins and destinations, namely that manual jobs are predominantly filled by sons of manual workers and, to a slightly lesser extent, that non-manual jobs recruit disproportionately from sons of non-manual fathers. It is the former type of occupation that has, on the whole, been contracting during most of this century, and the latter which has been expanding. Since these dominate the types of occupational change, this strongly affects any *measures* of change. For instance, the probability of being born middle class has increased, and so have the chances of a middle-class son getting a middle-class job: the ratio of the two probabilities (as in the odds – ratio extensively used in the Nuffield Study) reflects both changes.

There is no need to get into detailed discussion here, but as a rough guide, the overall trend in Britain since 1921 has been an expansion of non-manual employment from being about 30 per cent of the male labour force to about over 45 per cent in 1971. Spread over fifty years the change is not very great: if sons follow fathers into work some twenty years later, their opportunity structure is on average only around 6 per cent more non-manual than their fathers'. Of course specific occupations were greatly affected, others less so, and there has been no single historical trend, which further complicates the picture.

These arguments are predicated on the explicit premise that the mechanisms of selection do not change, but this is an assumption that has more heuristic value than empirical reality. In the first place, the spread of universal post-primary education means that more people have the qualifications to take non-manual jobs, and as Little and Westergaard among others have argued, the middle classes have done better out of this education boom than the working classes. As education is certainly a selection mechanism for many expanding occupations, the sons of the middle class have improved their competitive position for entry *vis-à-vis* the sons of the working class. In the second place, the relative expansion of one sector draws off recruits who might otherwise have competed for places at a lower level. This leaves the mechanisms of selection in the second – or in the generalised case, all other – occupational group(s) working on different 'human materials'. We would therefore expect the reproduction of the original patterns of recruitment to be somewhat distorted, because all occupational groups are changing at the same time.

For these several reasons, it is not possible to 'explain' mobility, in the sense of making precise predictive statements, on the basis of occupational change. It remains an empirical question to investigate what the consequences for mobility patterns may be. Equally, the operation of the selective mechanisms, for example education, remains part of the explanatory model, because we wish to know not just *how many* men from a particular origin have been recruited, but *why these men* rather than others from the same origins have been recruited. Thus the traditional interest in English mobility analysis, access to education, is not lost: rather it is balanced by the introduction of occupation on the demand side of the demand/supply function.

The change in 'occupational demand' is not the only element which a concern with occupation introduces. The distribution of occupations between regions and industrial sectors, the rate of technological change in each, and the shape of local labour markets help to identify the constraints of an individual's 'choice' of occupation. The mechanisms of knowing about vacancies, deciding whether a post is attractive, and the way fathers are able to intervene directly in the hiring process provide links between the structural framework and the life chances of the individual actor. To the extent that these are patterned by changes in 'occupational demand', which is an empirical question, they represent elaborations of the basic relationship, not all of which can be dealt with here.

The point has already been made that this is a shift in emphasis as compared, say, with Glass's focus on education as the key mechanism. It is also a shift in the way in which stratification is linked to social mobility. Most mobility research has concentrated on the argument that when mobility occurs, it does something to the stratification system. What the present study attempts to do is to extend the normal chain of connections, which may be represented as in Figure 2.1. Compared with earlier studies, we wish to emphasise the first of these connections. In fact, the present account goes beyond this, although only a partial and indicative way, to suggest other links in the chain, as in Figure 2.2.

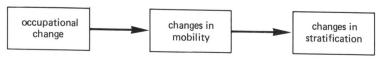

Figure 2.1 Conventional relationship between occupation and mobility

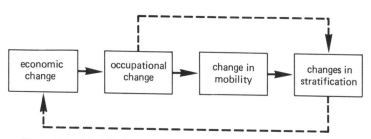

Figure 2.2 Modified relationship between occupation and mobility

First, occupations do not change autonomously. Occupations depend on the use of labour in the production of goods and services by organisations. These organisations are controlled by social actors who deploy capital, new technology, and other factors of production in pursuit of their goals. This economic process creates or destroys occupational opportunity.

Second, changes in occupations do not just affect stratification through mobility. Improvement in the market position of an occupational group improves its financial standing, while deskilling of its tasks degrades it. This direct effect is represented by the upper dotted line in Figure 2.2 not because it is unimportant, but because the present study is less concerned with that kind of ʾationship, important though it is.

The lower dotted line in Figure 2.2 connecting changes in stratification to economic change is a reminder that few relationships work purely in one direction. An example of this connection is the argument that the new middle class created by occupational change will adopt a set of political and social priorities stressing communal rather than profit-maximising goals. Expressed in contemporary terms, this would be support for public expenditure rather than cuts or privatisation of state operations. The use of the dotted line in Figure 2.2 as before indicates a legitimate and interesting line of connection, but one which does not take a central place in the present work. Other such lines could be added, for example connecting economic change directly to changes in stratification to take account of changes in property and modes of production.

However, it will be recognised that here our main emphasis is on the link between occupation and stratification. That is not to say that stratification is totally a product of occupation, but rather that this study is about occupations rather than say, property, or status, or the relations between classes. Necessarily the aspect of stratification which receives attention here is the economic one, so that 'classes' are empirically defined as aggregates of occupations, and class positions are chiefly conceptualised in terms of market and work situations. Other views of class, stressing 'struggle' or *the dynamic* created by the opposition of class interests, therefore receive little attention.

Despite this, Figure 2.2 as it stands is not tied to a single theoretical framework. With minor changes of wording the figure would be compatible with several competing positions. The basic structure of the connections would be almost as acceptable to such varied writers as Bell, Dahrendorf or Wright. The next step must therefore be to locate the core process of connections in a wider framework of ideas.

Broadly speaking, Marxist writers have argued that an explanation of class must be sought in the mode of production, and therefore concentrated their efforts on that feature. Johnson (1977), for example, has criticised the Weberian tradition for taking the market in which property and labour are sold as given, and thereby for failing to see that the value of skills depends on the needs of the mode of production. Crompton and Gubbay (1977) identify the extraction of surplus value as the key process, which turns the market into a system of exploitation. In this view, both Marxist and non-Marxist accounts can be heavily economic in emphasis, but the former claims to have identified a more fundamental level of explanation. Non-Marxists, such as Parkin (1979), tend to find the connections between the mode of production and the complexity of modern society hard to substantiate. They therefore draw on a wider range of economic forces (technology, knowledge skills, income) to account for a social world which increasingly is seen as departing from a two-class model of society.

In order to structure these different theoretical positions, it is necessary to make a somewhat arbitrary division between 'theories of capitalist society' and 'theories of industrial society'. Broadly speaking, the former draw on Marx, and attach varying degrees of primacy to the search for profit and control of the market exchange system, and to the historical process of class struggle. The latter stress the growing application of inanimate power to production, and the consequent new forms of social relationships associated with large-scale organisations and the factory system. Both approaches deal historically with changing occupational structures as part of a wider social process, but, given that mobility is seen largely as a product of occupational change, how are we to explain occupational change itself? The two schools adopt different views.

It is for this reason that we have chosen to contrast 'capitalist' with 'industrial' theories, rather than the more common Marxist versus Weberian distinction (Abercrombie and Urry, 1982; Scott, 1979). The latter distinction owes more to the debate about class, in which mobility as occupational change is a relevant but subsidiary part, whereas the differentiation used here brings out the occupational dimension more directly. It will be necessary to extract elements from that debate and even at times to relocate individual contributions in an unusual context, but the main focus of the present work makes this desirable.

Any discussion of these 'schools' of course disguises the internal complexity of debate that each contains. A prior, if only partial, consideration of each theory in its own terms and with its own internal disagreements is needed in order that those features which are directly related to mobility can be identified, in order to inform our analysis. This is seen as a step in the direction of re-establishing connections between mobility and several of the major themes of sociological theory, as a counter balance to mobility's present isolation as a sub-problem of social stratification.

3 Occupations in Capitalist Society

The theory of capitalist society not only has its origins in Marx's work, but much of the contemporary debate (for example, about the new middle classes) is tied to the detail of his writing and frequently refers back to Marx for legitimation. This chapter therefore begins by examining how Marx accounts for the core characteristics of modern society, particularly those relating to labour, and then goes on to discuss certain aspects of subsequent development of Marxist ideas. Necessarily, the version of these theories presented will be truncated and selective, because the prime focus of the present study is occupational change and mobility, rather than class struggle or the complex abstract models of modes of production which are central to Marxism.

The initial step is to characterise the main elements of the theory of capitalist society, drawing attention to its conception of work and class relations, and concentrating on Marx's ideas about changes in the middle strata. This is followed by a discussion of two specific sub-themes, to which Marxist and neo-Marxist sociologists have made important contributions; the nature of the new middle classes, and the debate over technology and the degradation of labour. These sub-themes again receive a less extensive treatment than if we were interested in them for their own sake.

HISTORICAL CHANGES IN LABOUR

We may begin by acknowledging the essentially historical style of the theory of capitalist society. As a result of its proponents' concern to show the uniqueness of modern modes of production, considerable attention has been paid to earlier social forms. From this it is possible to draw an important if somewhat general observation about the variety of ways in which labour has been organised in production. Mobility research assumes the 'freedom' of the individual to change jobs, and perhaps more crucially, not to follow in his father's footsteps, but this is dependent on the existence of contemporary forms of labour.

For example, under feudalism, the labour force typically consisted of serfs, free neither to determine their masters, their own movements,

30

their own work tasks, nor the form in which their rents were paid to the lord. In a low technology, simple economy, this applied to the vast majority. Even outside of the agricultural system, in the new towns whose growth contributed to the decline of feudalism, labour was not free (see Anderson, 1974; Wallerstein, 1974; Hill, 1969). There, the medieval guild system of production differed from that of feudal servility, because master, journeyman, and apprentice typically lived and worked together as a domestic unit. Nevertheless, the master retained strong paternalistic control, and the distinctions between the grades of labour were very marked. In particular, progress from journeyman to master was restricted by the guild's regulation of trade, and the frustration of the journeyman (over what we might reinterpret as blocked mobility) was ultimately one of the pressures that helped to undermine the system. The rigidity of the guild system did not just limit sideways and upward movement of labour; as urban growth continued, the guilds were unable to meet expanded demand for their products.

The mode of production that replaced the guild system was based on the merchant capitalist 'putting out' his work; providing the raw materials for families of out-workers who used their own tools in their own homes to manufacture goods which were then returned to the merchant for sale. The master/journeyman/apprentice paternalism was thus replaced by a simpler cash relationship, but one in which the outworkers retained some control over production. Recent writers have seen this as a central issue in the introduction of the factory system. While factory production does allow the introduction of large-scale, inanimate sources of power (such as the water mill or steam engine) its attraction lies in overcoming what, from the merchant's point of view, were three defects of home-based work, namely:

> the lack of control by the merchant-capitalist over his workers; the economic losses through waste and fraud; and the uncertain nature of the labour force. The independent, voluntary status of the worker was slowly eroded in an attempt to increase the efficiency of exploitation, first, by allowing the worker to get into debt and, second, by taking away the worker's ownership of his tools. These two factors opened the way for the emergence of a class of alienable wage-labourers dependent on the capitalist class for both a living and a livelihood. (Clegg and Dunkerley, 1980, p. 50)

In this view, the industrial revolution, with its new technology and organisation, has no meaning except as the 'successful' outcome of the efforts of the capitalist class to establish its domination of society, to shape the social order (by controlling state machinery and other ideological apparatus) to suit its ends, and to develop new forms of capital accumulation. Under industrial capitalism, those who have no means of production must sell their labour as best they can on a market which is determined by the capitalist's purchase of labour for the production of their chosen products. Beyond that basic contract, there is nothing: worker/capitalist relationships are impersonal. To put it another way, workers are in principle free to change jobs and to obtain the best job they can, within a market where jobs are being created and destroyed by the capitalists through their control over the technology of production, and also over decisions about whether production itself should continue or cease. Feudal, guild, and out-work labour are replaced by a system in which social mobility, at least *within* a single broad class, and subject to market constraints, is possible.[1]

The underlying impersonality of the relationship between capital and labour is also further determined by the form of the business enterprise in modern capitalism. The rise of the joint stock company separated the capitalist from the enterprise itself; his ownership remained but his control was exercised indirectly (and some would argue, less effectively, e.g. Burnham, 1945) through the persons of managers and the legal entitlements of 'money capital', that is shares and bonds, etc. By means of one company controlling another, in increasing chains, the distance between the capitalist and the actual productive activity was extended. At the same time, a banking apparatus was required to handle the expanding workings of a joint-stock system, which helped to change the function of the banks from small borrowing and lending concerns into major forces which themselves exerted control over production.

> The central theme of the theory of capitalist society is the dominance of finance capital. Lenin and Bukharin both point to the fact that monopolized capital in banking and manufacturing fuses into 'finance capital' i.e. capital which is not restricted to one particular sphere of activity. (Scott, 1979, p. 24)

This process hastens the 'inevitable outcome of the nature of capitalism' (Aaronovitch, 1955, p. 14), that is the growth of monopoly capitalism, in which production is dominated by fewer and fewer, larger and larger enterprises. The banking and managerial apparatus needed for monopolistic corporations consists of new technological forms, manifested in occupations requiring new skills. Indeed, some jobs involve day-to-day control of the corporation and its other employees.

But that does not introduce any fundamental change in the basic relations of production.

> After all, the real power over production remains with the owners and not with those who in their name are directing technological progress, etc. The engineers and clerical employees of a monopolistic company cannot throw its owners out nor force them to surrender a portion of the profits in favour of the workers. The owners, on the other hand, can hire and fire engineers and clerical workers and dictate their will just as they could a hundred years ago. (Kuusinen *et al.*, 1959, p. 292)

Nor, as Mills has pointed out, can the manager automatically pass on his advantageous position to his children. They in turn must struggle for their own advance as he did before them (Mills, 1963). Real power remains in the hands of 'a few hundred or at most a few thousand men of wealth' (Perlo, 1957, p. 13).

However, the separation of ownership from direct control, together with the growth in the scale of organisations, the introduction of complex new technologies, and the need for an apparatus of ideological legitimation all require a different kind of wage labourer. This new middle class ranges from the top managers of major corporations, whose services are progressively rewarded with gifts of shares until they are effectively absorbed into the capitalist class, to some kind of clerical workers (for example, machine operators in Californian banks) whose pay, conditions, and skills have been eroded to the point that their work is indistinguishable from manual labour (Braverman, 1974). 'The middle class' is a misleading title: it is only *one* class in the sense that it lies between the capitalist class and the class of manual labourers, and that, in the theory of capitalist society, it owes its being to the forces of capital accumulation inherent in monopoly capitalism. But the diversity of its composition is such that it would be more accurate to talk about the middle *classes*. This not only reflects the internal differentiation of status that the incumbents themselves acknowledge, but also goes some way towards recognising that different occupational groups owe their existence to different aspects of the capitalist process. These points will be elaborated later in this chapter.

It is the emergence and massive growth of the new middle classes which provides the major opportunity for social mobility in capitalist society, although it is the more fundamental relationship between labour and capital which 'frees' the worker to be a mobile agent in the marketplace.

MARX AND MOBILITY

It might be expected from this conceptual basis that Marxist sociologists would have investigated social mobility extensively. Some writers on class in Britain, (for instance Westergaard and Resler, 1977), have used the findings of earlier studies in a limited way, but that apart, there has been little empirical, and not much more theoretical, work on mobility from the standpoint of the theory of capitalist society (two exceptions are Smith, 1983, and Robinson and Kelley, 1979). On the contrary, one of the more important recent accounts of social mobility in England and Wales (Goldthorpe, 1980a) starts with a lengthy defence against those on the left who see this kind of work as ideological support for the capitalist system.

Goldthorpe acknowledges that evidence of mobility patterns can be used ideologically, and the opening chapter of *Social Mobility and Class Structure in Modern Britain* devotes considerable effort to the identification of 'interests' in writing on social mobility: that is to say, to relating various styles of social mobility analysis to the positions that key figures have taken on the subject of the class structure of capitalist societies in particular, and capitalism in general. While this can be justified as a means of clarifying sub-schools within mobility analysis, its explicit rationale (Goldthorpe, 1980a, pp. 2–3) is as a direct response to the Marxist critique that a concern with social mobility is inherently bourgeois. Furthermore, its treatment of the selected key figures is uneven: the attention devoted to Marx is unjustified except in terms of a perceived need to placate a potentially hostile audience on the Left.

Thus, we find the first nine pages concentrating on a demonstration of the fact that Karl Marx did in fact deal with social mobility. Fourteen direct references or quotations are introduced between pages 4 and 9, with the sources ranging from the *Manifesto*, through the *Eighteenth Brumaire*, and *Theories of Surplus Value*, to *Capital*. Although there are only two direct references to it, Goldthorpe appears to be drawing heavily on Harris (1939), whose work Goldthorpe calls the outstanding critical contribution to the study of intermediate strata in Marx's work (Goldthorpe 1980a, p. 32). Goldthorpe uses this evidence to challenge the more accepted view propagated by Van Heek (1956, p. 131): 'Nineteenth century liberalism was blind to the problem (of mobility): Marxism attached little importance to it.' But as Goldthorpe himself has to admit:

> while Marxism no less than liberalism thus foreclosed on the question of mobility, the further point that we would wish to bring out here is

that, *so far as Marx's own writings are concerned*, the significance of
mobility is in fact a good deal greater than has usually been supposed.
*It is true that Marx discussed mobility directly only, as it were, in the
context of other problems, and then at no great length.* (Goldthorpe
1980a, p.4 – first emphasis original, second added)

This presents us with the dubious argument that Marx may have
written almost nothing about the subject, but that it had great 'covert
significance' in his work (Goldthorpe 1980a, p. 4). We must therefore
decide whether Marx saw the true significance of mobility and yet
capriciously chose *not* to write much about it, or whether he in fact only
partially saw it as a problem, mistook its true importance for future
developments, and so paid it scant attention. (See also Crompton and
Gubbay's sceptical comment, 1977, p. 47.)

If we are to believe Goldthorpe, Marx did appreciate the importance
of mobility, despite writing almost nothing about it in the whole of his
prolific output. Two consequences follow from this position. First,
Goldthorpe has established that mobility can be analysed from any
ideological standpoint, not just from that of the apologist for capitalism.
Second, he has established a hallowed, symbolic pedigree for the study
of social mobility: if Marx himself sanctified it, we may all safely follow
in his footsteps. Goldthorpe goes on to discuss several post-Marxist
writers who, he is able to demonstrate, use mobility as a means of
elaborating aspects of Marx's work. Thus Bernstein deals with the fate
of the lesser classes, or strata, caught between the two major forces of the
bourgeoisie and the proletariat; Sombart grows pessimistic about the
fate of socialism in an affluent and mobile society like the USA – a kind
of society not fully anticipated by Marx; and Michels deals with the way
mobility aspirations and achievements weaken the position of the
working class. Significantly, Goldthorpe's accounts show only that
these writers were in dialogue with Marx, not that they were in dialogue
specifically with the fourteen quoted references where Marx spoke
directly on social mobility.

This same caveat must be entered in the case of four more
recognisable contributors to social mobility; Sorokin, Lipset, Glass and
Duncan. While Goldthorpe skilfully disentangles the differences in
interest and emphasis that distinguish these four sociologists, he is
unable to show how they responded to Marx's view of social mobility.
Indeed, it is apparent that their ideas are part of a non-Marxist critique
of capitalism, but in no way can be said to be a direct response to Marx
on mobility. These writers belong, as we shall see, to the theorists of
industrial society.

If, on the other hand, one rejects the Goldthorpe position that social mobility had some kind of 'covert significance' for Marx, where does this leave a Marxist view of mobility? It was suggested above that there is within the theory of capitalist society ample grounds for an explanation of mobility. Nevertheless, it is not a subject which has received much attention. In fact, social mobility as it occurs in modern capitalism seems to be a source of great embarrassment to Marxists. Its existence weakens class boundaries, dilutes class consciousness, and helps to explain the failure of Marx's prediction of proletarian revolution. Why have Marxists (apart from defectors like Sombart) not studied mobility?

First, as indicated in the previous chapter, some writers like Poulantzas lay so much stress on abstract structures of production that, in comparison, mobility of persons has no significance at all. Second, empirical analysis (except for historical analysis, where there is not much to be said about mobility) has not been a strong point of European, and particularly British, Marxism. Goldthorpe is right that mobility can be studied by sociologists of any ideological hue, but he fails to recognise that Marxist sociologists have shown themselves almost without exception to be able historians or theorists, but most unwilling to carry out systematic contemporary fieldwork (see Payne *et al.*, 1981, pp. 70–84). No amount of invocation of the Master's works will change this: it will remain far easier to label mobility analysis as bourgeois and so define it out of relevance.

However, this dearth of empirical sociological research is less important than the main point that social mobility in its modern sense fits uneasily with Marx's own conception of capitalism. Although he allowed for several minor strata between the bourgeoisie and the proletariat – such as state functionaries, small traders or industrial managers – and in numerous places acknowledges the existence of the middle classes, the main concentration of his argument was on the significance of the two major classes and the dominance of the one over the other.[2] If, unlike Goldthorpe, we choose to concentrate on this other element in Marx's work, then it becomes apparent that social mobility is an unresolved problem, particularly in his early writing (although see McLellan, 1973, pp. 13–25 for a discussion of 'periods' in Marx's writing).

In the first place, if one emphasises this dimension of Marx's work, and leaves to one side for the moment the new middle classes, the two classes are by definition separate and mutually antagonistic. It is possible for there to be limited downward social mobility, as a capitalist fails and is reduced to the ranks of the proletariat by the loss of his capital. It is harder to see how Marx's theory allows for the accumulation of capital to permit individual mobility in the reverse direction. In the longer term, the proletarian revolution will result in a kind of social mobility (although Marx did not think of it in such terms) when the ruling class is deposed and a classless equalitarian society is established. Until that day, all other movements between occupations are unimportant, and not to be described as social mobility, because by definition, almost all of them take place within a single occupational category, the working class.

It is slightly unusual to present Marx's conception of class in terms of occupational categories in this way. In non-Marxist discussions of how occupational categories are constructed, two main criteria, work task and associated rewards, stand out. In Marx's writing, members of the proletariat share the same relationships to the means of production; they sell their labour. Although the details of what labour they sell differ, it is not the *difference* that matters to Marx, it is the similarity of the conditions under which they sell, and the rewards that are thereby obtained. Thus 'work task', narrowly defined, is not a major part of Marx's conception; it is the exchange of labour for wages that matters. Differences in work tasks, or the technical division of labour, are reduced to a level of relative insignificance so that only the common act of 'work' remains. Thus all subtler occupational differences cannot count for social mobility unless some kind of false consciousness intervenes. In the same way, the rewards, both material and non-material, which accrue to different occupations, are treated as being undifferentiated except at the level of division between the two main classes.

This reading of Marx is the one adopted by one of the very few recent attempts to tackle mobility from a 'Marxian perspective' (Smith, 1983). Smith defines mobility as that between 'wage and salary workers' and what he calls the capitalist class (although he is somewhat inconsistent in his discussion of the petty bourgeoisie, the self-employed, managers, and proprietors). He is able to show using local data on Memphis in the USA that the capitalist class is shrinking and that movements between the two classes are declining. The shrinkage he attributes to the monopolisation of capital (he excludes managers), and the decline in mobility to the consequent structure of class opportunity. Robinson and Kelley (1979) also treat mobility as a measure of how ownership and control over the means of production is inherited, again taking the idea of two antagonistic classes as the main message from Marx (see also Hindess, 1981 and Johnson and Rattansi, 1981).

Mobility has then received little attention because what most sociologists regard as movement is, for the Marxist, contained within a single working class. Its relevance for Marxism is to demonstrate the separation of the capitalist class from the working class and to show that that separation is increasing because 'real' mobility is small and decreasing. Mobility could in principle also be used as an explanation for the generation of false consciousness, but that latter notion has not been at the centre of recent debate. Because most mobility research does not focus on either the capitalist class or false consciousness, mobility analysts of whatever political colour can be castigated as bourgeois ideologues who spend their time and effort in the study of a non-problem, so diverting the attention of others away from 'the real issues'.

If there *is* any room for some kind of mobility analysis in Marx's conception, it is one which draws on his discussion of the internal sub-divisions of the major classes and the ways these evolve. In other words, we can identify social mobility of a structural kind, in which entire classes or strata are elevated or depressed, or incorporated as adjuncts to another class. Significantly, the bulk of Goldthorpe's reference to social mobility in Marx's writing deals with just this. This is 'significant' in the sense that according to the present argument, it could not be otherwise, but also significant in that attempting to rehabilitate social mobility into Marxist sociology, Goldthorpe concentrates on structural mobility rather than other less palatable forms which represent a potentially greater challenge. There is a certain irony in this, because Goldthorpe's own mobility analysis often displays less interest in structural mobility than in exchange mobility.

Although Marx in no way offers a systematic treatment of the subject, his limited comments do point to one of the major themes of the present analysis, changes in the occupational structure. It is on the wholesale creation and destruction of strata that he remarks. Mackenzie (1982, p. 64) has argued that Marx pays little attention to the new middle classes because he sees them as historically transitional and therefore not important as they will disappear. In contrast, Abercrombie and Urry (1983) concentrate on the creation of new strata, emphasising Marx's prediction of growth made in *Capital*. They do, however, note that 'just what the political significance of a non-labour class constituting one-third or perhaps one-half of the population is', is left unstated by Marx (Abercrombie and Urry, 1983, p. 50) (see also Mackenzie, 1976 and Hodges, 1961).

Interestingly, these strata are far more differentiated and smaller than the two major classes. They are identified in terms of occupational groups with specialist work task functions, as much as in terms of their place in the class struggle, and certainly much more so than in discussions of the bourgeoisie and proletariat. Their 'mobility' is a collective one, encompassing a whole category, rather than a mobility of individuals: the collectivity is brought into existence by new technological and capitalist forces, or displaced by the rigours of capitalist development. Paradoxically, this is one of the points to which many critics have objected, namely that Marx made insufficient allowance for the extent of middle-class growth, and so misread the future lines of the class struggle (e.g. Sorokin, 1927; Berle and Means, 1932; Burnham, 1945).

In contrast, mobility analysis has traditionally concentrated on individual mobility, and attempted to control for the effects of changing occupational structures (although see Parry and Parry, 1977, p. 112) It has thus not taken on board, until recently, the potentially powerful insight that an expanded middle class offers mobility opportunities, because the new recruits are very likely to come from some other backgrounds at least in the first generation. This was something which Marx did not fully perceive.

To be fair to Marx, there are points in his work where he does seem to be aware of this phenomenon. In his discussion of recruitment to the expanded commercial office in *Capital*, vol. III, although emphasising that its ultimate effect is supportive of capital and damaging to wage levels, he writes:

> The generalisation of public education makes it possible to recruit this line of labourers [officer workers] from a class that had formerly no access to such education and that were accustomed to a lower scale of living. (Marx, 1959b, p. 354)

Harris (in whose 1939 work the above quotation was located by the author) demonstrates convincingly that Marx expected and accounted for a very considerable rise in the *dritte personen*: office staff[3]; commercial agents, such as buyers, sellers, and travellers; those involved in the calculation of prices, book-keeping, managing funds, carrying on correspondence; officials, parsons, professors, magistrates; soldiers, sailors, clerical employees, policemen, mistresses, clowns, and jugglers; artists, musicians, lawyers, physicians, professors, schoolmasters, inventors, commercial labourers, managers, salesmen, cashiers, and merchants. Why then is this new middle class ('new' in the sense that in much of Marx's writing, it was the capitalist class that was the old middle class between the landowners and the working class) not identified as a powerful historical force?

Harris explains this in two main ways. First, in understanding capitalism, it is to the dominant modes of production and class relations that the analyst must turn. Thus for example, the small-scale farmer or the worker on his own account are little more than an irrelevance: the fate of the petty bourgeoisie at the hands of the capitalist class will eventually tidy up such inconsistencies. Second, the newer middle class is also marginal, because its service 'does not incorporate itself in commodities and therefore, does not give rise to a surplus-product. It is unproductive labour which is performed outside the process of capitalist production' (Harris, 1939, p. 341).

Unproductive labour is the type of labour which does not create new value in the form of a surplus product. It is not a matter of whether there is a physical product or not, but rather whether it contributes to an increased profit for the capitalist. It is the giving of more labour time than is received back in wages that defines labour as productive. All other kinds of activity create use value, but not profit. Harris here seems to underestimate (in keeping with Marx?) the extent to which the new middle class is employed for profit, and therefore is productive.

This is a central 'point' in Marx's conception of modern capitalism. He regards most of the new middle class as marginal, because their labour has only use value: one part of it represents a response to the capitalist class's drift towards a lavish life-style with a system of retainers to service their needs; a second part of it (the 'functionaries in trade and marketing', Harris, 1939, p. 343) is helping only the circulation of commodities, which is not the essential element in capitalist production; and a third part is employed by the state, which makes no profit, and is again merely an enabling mechanism for capitalist production. At the same time, the survival of the petty bourgeoisie has been achieved by technological change which allows new markets to open up as temporary refuges before large-scale capital takes over each new activity. There is then no systematic sociology of the new middle class (and therefore of mobility) in Marx's own writing because the middle classes are devalued.

RECENT ACCOUNTS OF THE NEW MIDDLE CLASS

The vacuum left by Marx has been largely filled by Marxist writers in the last decade. Despite many protestations on their part that Marx did in fact take account of the middle class, the sheer volume of contributions to this debate is evidence that he did not provide a clear statement on the subject (see for example Nicolaus, 1967; Poulantzas, 1973; Braverman, 1974; Carchedi, 1975 and 1977; Wright, 1976 and 1978; Crompton and Gubbay, 1977; Hunt, 1977; Walker, 1979; Edwards, 1980; Mackenzie, 1982; Abercrombie and Urry, 1983). What is striking about all of these contributors is that as soon as they discuss in concrete form any class other than the property-owning class, they use *occupation* to identify membership. Thus, even though their prime concern would seem to lead them in one direction, in practice they are tied to occupations and occupational structures.

The debate has centred around the problem of identifying which, if any, of the classic classes is the true home of the new middle classes. To take several examples, Poulantzas, addressing the question of political strategy in France, has argued that they are a fraction of the petty bourgeoisie. Carchedi, on the other hand, proposes that they perform some functions of both labour and capital, while Nicolaus sees them as a consumption class separate from but contributing to productive labour. Ehrenreich and Ehrenreich (1979) take the view that the class of professionals and managers has to be seen as a separate class in its right, distinct from previous classes.

If the present study were adopting a specifically Marxist framework, it would be necessary to deal with this body of work in some detail, so that mobility into the new middle classes could be defined as upward, downward or sideways movements. As we are not tied to such a framework, the need for such an analysis does not arise, but it is nonetheless useful to consider briefly three features of these exchanges. First, what occupations are being talked about? Second, what criteria are used to distinguish between classes? And third, what explanations are used to explain the growth or decline of these classes (this being the most interesting element)?

Part of the disagreement between the leading protagonists can be traced to the level of discourse adopted. Because this has been mainly theoretical in nature, empirical reference points are sometimes hard to establish. Whereas Ehrenreich and Ehrenreich (1979) concentrate on professionals and managers, as distinct from other occupations, Poulantzas allocates senior managers to the capitalist class, and then combines the remaining administrators and professionals with hair-dressers, foremen, entertainers and other wage-earning groupings. His initial statement on the nature of the new petty bourgeoisie immediately moves into a discussion of the theory of surplus value and class polarisation (Poulantzas, 1975, pp. 204–30). Similarly Crompton and Gubbay (1977) find it possible to discuss the middle ground of occupations in terms of 'structural ambiguity' without specifying which occupations they have in mind: their development later emphasises the proletarianisation of technicians and clerks, rather than managers or professionals, which colours their account (1977, p. 171 and pp. 197–202). Wright's (1976; 1978) categorisation of the middle class in terms of ambiguous or contradictory structural locations pays less attention to technicians and clerks, although he does cover a wide range of occupations under his four groupings of upper managers, lower supervisors, small business men, and 'semi-autonomous wage earners'. This latter category is, however, not very satisfactory as it combines technicians, certain teachers, filling station owners, and other professionals because they are self-employed (Wright, 1976, pp. 20–35; 1978, pp. 63–88). Clerks are not part of the new middle class because they are non-autonomous, non-supervisory employees, a view shared by Baran (1957, pp. 32–3).

The 'class identification' or 'boundary' problem (Hunt, 1977, p. 10; Mackenzie, 1982, p. 63) thus takes three forms. First, it consists of arguments about the 'top' and 'bottom' of the new middle classes: are senior managers in the working or capitalist class? Second, it consists of (often implicit) emphasis on one or other subdivision, so that commentators often argue past one another. And third, it consists of confusions over the subdivisions of the remaining occupations, often due to lack of concrete examples in the exposition.

However, this confusion is also due to the particular aspects in Marxism to which a contributor connects his own argument, i.e. to the criteria employed to distinguish between classes and to identify their essential character. As this is not central to the main themes of the present study, we shall simply indicate several of the approaches adopted. A number of writers share more than one such approach. As against most non-Marxist accounts, which pay more attention to the empirical identification of each class, the theorists of capitalist society are concerned with how classes *interact*, and the part they play in the maintenance of the capitalist mode of production. Wright (for example, 1978, p. 64ff.), Carchedi (1977, ch. 1), Crompton and Gubbay (1977, ch. 9) and Braverman (1974, ch. 2) all stress the importance of control and authority. On the one hand, control and authority are relations between classes, and on the other they constitute functions by means of which capitalist reproduction is possible. The latter two writers are more concerned with the control aspects and draw pessimistic conclusions about proletarianisation. Like Wright and Carchedi, Ehrenreich and Ehrenreich are also concerned with reproduction, but they pay more attention to the cultural and ideological function. The professional and managerial class through the division of labour has appropriated mental labour from the proletariat, creating mutual antagonism, and while similarly having different class interest from the bourgeoisie, this class is now indispensable to capitalism because of its major function in 'the reproduction of capitalist culture and capitalist class relations' (Ehrenreich and Ehrenreich, 1979, p. 12).

A more political criterion is advocated by Hunt *et al.* (1977). In criticising economistic versions of Marxism, they draw on Marx's view of the importance of political and ideological factors, and see one central question as being what role the new middle class will play in the class struggle. The middle class's historical role in the proletarian revolution helps to define its character and form.

Finally, Poulantzas (together with others such as Crompton and Gubbay) uses Marx's theory of surplus values to identify the 'true' place of the new middle class. A clear insistence on a distinction between productive and non-productive labour is used to mark off certain occupations as neither bourgeois nor proletarian. This attaches the idea of occupation and class very closely to elements of economic thinking in Marx, which is somewhat restrictive.

One problem with this approach is that it forces contemporary economic activities, such as the greatly expanded public and commercial sectors, into a nineteenth-century manufacturing mould. It is not clear, for example, why Carchedi's definition of the collective labourer deals only with productive labour, or why Poulantzas restricts productive labour to the production of material goods: while these decisions may be consistent with earlier economic theory, they take little account of the volume of contemporary economic activity that is excluded, and thereby build in a complication for conceptualising class. Equally, it is not clear why the realisation of surplus value, either at the level of the individual enterprise or at the social level is diminished by the extension of circulation through the commercial chain, since at each level the value of the product is enhanced by distribution and retail agents. Nor is it an adequate answer to criticism of the productive/non-productive distinction that 'objections to it on the grounds that it is unrealistic, irrational or inconsistent are properly directed against capitalism itself' (Kay, 1979, p. 133).

Having sketched in some of the variation in conceptions of the new middle classes, we can now deal with explanations given for the growth of these classes in capitalist society. In general most writers have spent less time on this point, relying on either a commonsense view that the new middle classes exist and therefore are to be analysed, or on brief reference to some of Marx's own ideas. This can have slightly bizarre effects: despite his rhetoric that classes are created and take their being from the class struggle, Poulantzas offers very little concrete historical evidence to show how the new petty bourgeoisie have evolved out of struggle. His core explanation is that the logic of capitalist competition generates needs for new technical methods of production: the new technology is dependent on those who have high levels of scientific knowledge and others who control the more complex processes of production that become necessary. Poulantzas therefore illustrates three of the main themes in explaining the rise of the new middle class. At a basic level, he identifies the pursuit of surplus value as the driving force, while knowledge and control become the two functional foci of the new class.

To these can be added Johnson's (1977) argument that the growth of the state and its enhanced role in regulating and reproducing labour power requires new functionaries whose position is dependent on the control of knowledge itself. Ehrenreich and Ehrenreich make something of the same point, and also stress the reorganisation of the production process and the commodification of working-class life as sources of the professional and managerial class. Like Nicolaus, they further note the need for a condition of surplus to support such a class, but not to the extent of adopting his view that its capacity for consumption is necessary for the continuance of capitalism. In contrast, Carchedi locates the key process in the need for control and surveillance in the work place in order to produce surplus value under monopoly capitalism. Finally, Wright draws on the alternative tradition, the 'theory of industrial society' to highlight the effect of sectoral shift in industrial activity as the specific source of the new middle classes. We can thus identify both technical and exploitative forces as ultimate causes, with the processes of technical knowledge control, of production (commodification, consumption and service), of ideological control (state regulation) and of control in the work places all being seen as immediate causes of an expanded middle class.

Abercrombie and Urry (1983, pp. 95–9) have recently given a more comprehensive statement of the causes of middle-class growth based on four main developments. They start in the sphere of circulation with the growth in *working-class consumption power*, arguing that this has generated new production activities. These entail the manufacture of more complex commodities, and the provision of new services, both commercial (e.g. leisure) and social, as in the case of health and education. The organisation of these activities, as well as the tasks to be performed, calls forth a new differentiated body of middle-class personnel.

Their second area of development is in the sphere of production, typified by the *growth of the service sector*. This has been fuelled by the availability of capital, which can be used to meet the need to research markets and plan future investment in a sophisticated way, so establishing commercial services. In parallel, consumer services have expanded through technological innovation: whether as entertainment (computer games) or health care (computer diagnosis), the range of occupational opportunities in conception, planning, marketing and servicing are vastly increased. This overlaps to some extent with their third driving force, *the faster turnover of fixed capital*. Due to advanced technology, high rates of obsolescence create technical and research employment, while the combination of high investment and rapid obsolescence puts a premium on forward planning.

The final source of the new middle class lies more directly in the field of *class struggle*. The success of working-class movements like trade unionism provokes an apparatus of managerial and state employees whose function is to contain the increasingly professionalised forces representing the working class. The expansion of the state is a response designed to dominate the 'sphere of reproduction'.

These changes yield not a single class, but a category of labour with complex class functions in a wide range of activities and a variety of production settings and small capital units. They may be differentiated by virtue of the four sources of changes that brought them into being, but they share a common feature in possessing knowledge and educational qualifications (although see Abercrombie and Urry's reservations about credentialism, 1983, pp. 111–12). The sub-sets of the new middle class are capable of entering into class struggle with each other, as well as against other classes: their situation is essentially fluid, so that any discussion of their role must take account of historical processes. For example, although Abercrombie and Urry stress the expansion of the middle class, by which they actually seem mainly to mean the professional and managerial class, they accept the thesis of the proletarianisation of white collar workers provided it is seen as a long-term process (1983, p. 118).

This brings us to one of the other major themes in the theory of capitalist society, proletarianisation. In the foregoing discussion this was at times somewhat arbitrarily ignored, for reasons of simplifying the exposition (for example in presenting Poulantzas' ideas). However, the argument that the middle classes are expanding has almost as strong a counter argument that the constituent occupations are undergoing deskilling and increased control in the technical process of production (a point not irrelevant to our earlier claim that different writers have often concentrated on particular fractions of the middle class to the exclusion of others). The proletarianisation thesis is mainly concerned with production and control, and can be presented largely through a brief discussion of Braverman and his critics.

TECHNOLOGY AND OCCUPATIONAL CHANGE

In contrast to the theorists of industrial society, who have stressed the creation of new and demanding occupations and the general upgrading of skill levels in modernisation (see Chapters 4 and 5), several theorists of capitalist society have in the last few years dwelt on the thesis of labour deskilling. Braverman's (1974) *Labour and Monopoly Capitalism* is a key text here, while the control aspects of this process have been developed by Marglin (1974), Clegg and Dunkerley (1980) and Salaman (1979). It is the former which most concerns us here, but the other contributions are mentioned to provide a proper representation of the argument in its entirety.

Braverman starts with the paradox that modern work is said, on the one hand, to require 'ever higher levels of education, training, the greater exercise of intelligence and mental effort in general' while, on the other hand, it is said to be 'mindless, bureaucratised and alienating' (Braverman, 1974, pp. 3–4). Rather than welcoming the division of labour as did earlier writers, he regards the subdivision of work into specialist and unskilled tasks as a retrograde step. The effect of Scientific Management was 'to strip the workers of craft knowledge and autonomous control and confront them with a fully thought-out process in which they function as cogs and levers' (1974, p. 136). The result is an increase in control by the employer, a reduction in discretion and autonomy on the part of the worker, and the further alienation of the work force. The subsequent rapid advance of science and technology to a central place in the operation of monopoly capitalism did nothing to reverse this process of dehumanisation and deskilling because the new technological processes were not only 'Taylorised' into trivial work inputs from the outset, but also demanded less labour *per se*. As machines become more sophisticated, the need for skilled operators is reduced.

Braverman reviews each of the major categories of occupation in turn. Skilled manual work, in the sense of craft labour, is the centrepiece of his argument, because it has existed throughout the hundred or so years with which he deals. Drawing on a wide range of sources, he demonstrates how craft labour has been largely replaced by workers who, while retaining craft titles, in fact neither have, nor are called upon to use, craft skills. Office workers, being a relatively recent phenomenon of the twentieth century have been recruited from the ranks of women, and their tasks almost from the outset have been devised on scientific management lines. Braverman regards the semi-skilled workers as merely a census statistician's creation, having no basis in genuine task analysis, and virtually indistinguishable from 'unskilled' labour. The ranks of management are also to be regarded with scepticism since they include many occupations which in fact discharge little in the way of truly managerial duties. The 'upgrading' of occupations in this century is seen as an illusion.

Although Braverman's view was at first received favourably, it has since attracted a number of criticisms (see Wood, 1982, p. 12). Braverman is overdependent on the general applicability of Taylorism, whereas the complexity of skill and work tasks makes it difficult to treat deskilling as a unitary process (King *et al.*, 1981). What counts as skill is not a given but a socially constructed phenomenon, while the process of deskilling may not only start from a historical position where the artisan is not the typical worker, but will take different forms in the course of management struggles with organised labour (see the contributions of Elger, Penn, Little, and More in Wood, 1982, and Edwards, 1980). The use of skills may vary both geographically between regional elements of an enterprise, while employment in the state apparatus where different imperatives operate limits the extent to which US production and commercial situations can be generalised to the whole of modern capitalism (Abercrombie and Urry, 1983, pp. 57–8).

Despite these several limitations, it is still worth asking whether any part of his argument applies to Britain. Almost all of Braverman's examples are drawn, not unnaturally, from his own country, namely the USA. While certain similarities exist between the USA and Britain, can we assume that the same pattern applies to both? For one thing, Britain has not experienced the waves of peasant immigration that the USA has, while a different imperial role, earlier industrialisation, and a stronger trade union movement are all plausible potential reasons why occupational change could take a different form in Britain. It must be said that there is some evidence that Braverman's argument can be applied to Britain. He himself quotes Lockwood (1958) on the blackcoated worker in his own support, while Davies (1979, p. 175) has recently reported deskilling in three samples of craftsmen, steel workers and office staff. Crompton (1980), in an explicit reference to Braverman and social mobility, claims that changes in clerical work have not just degraded the clerk, but that some apparently managerial employment has been devalued, since it consists only of what was previously clerical work. She makes a parallel case for draughtsmen, and to a less extent, for computer-related jobs (1980, 118–9).

On the other hand, as Goldthorpe (1980b) comments in his reply, the relative lack of general evidence over large numbers of occupations probably indicates that there is only a small number of exceptional cases (1980b, pp. 122–23). Gallie, in discussing large-scale, high automated plant, identifies an early period in which there was 'specialisation of the work task, with its concomitants of a sharp reduction in skill levels', but concludes that 'automation reversed the trend towards an ever-increasing division of labour'. With labour costs now a relatively much smaller proportion of total costs there was less need to extract so much from the labour force (Gallie, 1978, pp. 7–9). Jones (1982) and Penn (1982b) have shown how in engineering and textiles workers were in some cases even able to enhance their skills. Prandy *et al.* (1982, p. 182) are also sceptical about deskilling among white collar workers. And Roberts (1978), after discussing the deskilling thesis, concludes that on the basis of British studies 'it is doubtful that an aggregated impression would justify talk of a wholesale degradation of manual work' (1971, p. 45). While we cannot produce evidence on job content, it is possible to examine whether new, *relatively* more skilled occupations have been created this century, to balance any degradation of existing jobs, and this is done in Chapter 5.

In the meantime, Braverman's thesis poses three kinds of problem for social mobility analysis. In the first place, his argument that the work tasks of any given occupation have changed means that historical comparisons – son's occupation with his father's – must be highly suspect. Does it mean the same thing if father and son were both 'skilled manual workers'? If the occupation has been deskilled, does this depress the position of the occupation in the occupational hierarchy? For Braverman this is not a problem, since following Marx he regards all of these non-capitalist class jobs as proletarian. But for the mobility analyst who believes such a crude categorisation is too great an oversimplification, Braverman's argument is a further facet of the basic problem of historical comparison. A period which has seen the demise of the horse-drawn omnibus driver and the domestic servant and the rise of the computer programmer and the television producer (and for that matter, the professional sociologist) contains so much occupational change as to pose a threat to the basic operational approach of occupational mobility. What Braverman's work does is not just to add more evidence of such changes, but to show it applies throughout the occupational structure, and that any hierarchical ordering of occupations over a period of half a century may well be subject to distortion.

The second problem which Braverman poses is one central to this thesis, namely how far is it true that there has been a change in occupations such that an increase in upward mobility is possible. According to Braverman, no such change has taken place: most of the alleged new middle classes are in fact middle class in appearance alone. The new occupations are as proletarian as any of the deskilled manual jobs. His evidence on office work is very strong on this, but less so for other middle-class jobs: for example, his census data are somewhat undifferentiated. Further discussion is obviously desirable, but it must wait until we have seen what the rival theory of industrial society has to say on the matter.

Braverman's third problem is a conceptual one, which takes us back to our initial comments on class and occupation. His work is motivated by a deep humanist concern with the plight of the worker, not only exploited by the capitalist but controlled by him down to the minutest level of task performance. Thus questions of autonomy and alienation assume a major importance in how he conceives of an occupation. As Dunkerley has observed,

> the working class is involved in the execution and not the conception of tasks. The working class is controlled; the middle class, as agents of capital, control the labour process. (Dunkerley, 1979, 15)

It follows that deskilling is not just task-specific degradation, but deals with patterns of relationships; authority, seniority, superordination, autonomy. It is here that Braverman's thesis comes closest to other accounts of proletarianisation, like those of Carchedi, Baran and to a lesser extent, Wright. Therefore the degradation of the alleged middle class or any upgrading of skill levels must be measured not just in terms of formal titles or qualification, i.e. mobility studies using survey data cannot provide a complete answer. This difference of emphasis is not just a matter of technique, it is a question of which dimensions of class identity receive most attention, and therefore appear to be pre-eminent, i.e. it is also a theoretical question.

Indeed, it would be more accurate to say that the differences arise out of fundamental assumptions about the world. The idea of deskilling and technological control under monopoly capitalism is based in a critique of capitalism, whereas the notion of technology as creator of ever new (occupational) opportunities draws, as we shall see in the next chapter, on the theory of industrial society. Much of the debate about the role of technology has been carried out in the literature dealing specifically with organisational theory rather than with wider issues and not connected with mobility research. For example, some writers have stressed the pre-eminence of technology, such as Sayles (1958) on work group types or Woodward (1965) on management structures. Others. like Clegg and Dunkerley (1980), have argued that the presentation of technology as a neutral, rational, progressive force serves the ideological function of legitimating not just increased managerial control over the worker (in line with Braverman's thesis) but also the continued drive to profit maximisation.

Following Marglin (1976) they suggest that

> the most efficient technology (in terms of the maximum production) will be chosen only if it is compatible with securing the maximum control over worker behaviour. The corollary of this is that the attempt to gain greater control may result in a less efficient or productive technological system being employed. (Clegg and Dunkerley, 1980, p. 343)

Even though they do not substantiate this claim with empirical evidence, their orientation is important because it so directly challenges the notion of technology as simple and irresistible 'efficiency'. For them, technology and work are an aspect of class *relations*: in most mobility analysis, drawing as it does on a different theoretical tradition, *occupation is used only as an indicator of class position*. The alternative theoretical framework is discussed in the next two chapters.

4 Occupations in Post-Industrial Society

The theory of industrial society differs from the theory of capitalist society in the pre-eminence it gives to the processes inherent in production based on a complex technology. The essence of its argument is that modern society is a unique form, not just because it has at its disposal this technology, but also because the kinds of social organisation which are compatible with high technology represent a distinctive set in their own right. Therefore an explanation of industrial society must be based on an understanding of its particular characteristics, and take account of the logical imperatives that are part of a science-based society. Some writers have stressed the rationality of such societies and their superiority in terms of their efficiency in providing material rewards for their citizens. Others have interposed value systems as the connection between technology and social structure and, in a more ideological vein during the later 1950s and early 1960s, argued for the moral superiority of (US) pluralistic democratic industrial society over other social orders. More recent versions have used the label of 'post-industrial' society to identify the way in which control over knowledge, and the operation of a service economy, lead to new political and class allegiances. Thus the pursuit of profit and its consequent exploitative class relations which are the pivots of capitalist society theory, are replaced by the rational, neutral forces of technology as the central common core of theories of industrial society.

WHAT IS INDUSTRIAL SOCIETY?

One of the peculiar features of the theory of industrial society is that it contains relatively few precise statements of what an industrial society is actually like. There are some discussions of cases which indicate that the society under analysis is industrial (for example, Touraine's (1974) account of France in the 1960s), while most contributors deal in a general way with industrialisation as the process which gives rise to industrial society. But these provide only implicit statements about industrial society *per se*, which tend to be diffuse and unsystematic. Aron's (1967a) own questions in *The Industrial Society* still go largely unanswered:

How are we to define industrial society? Is the term appropriate? Is there not already such a thing as post-industrial society? Where exactly, at the present moment, do the essential differences between the two types of society occur, and how significant are these differences? . . . Where does the so-called industrial society begin and end? From what point are we entitled to call a society industrial? None of these questions admits of a categorical answer. (Aron, 1967a, pp. 97 and 105)

Not surprisingly, there is disagreement over which nations fit the bill: Lenski (1970), for example, lists twenty-five 'selected' industrial societies including Spain, Ireland and Greece as 'marginal cases' in 1967. Elsewhere he lists twenty-seven cases for 1964, based on annual per capita coal equivalent consumption (Lenski, 1970, pp. 347 and 325–2). Holt and Turner (1970, p. 10) meanwhile assert that on 'any commonly held definitions' there are only eight to twelve industrial societies in 1970. Again, Kumar (1974, p. 352) in a slightly more elaborated model uses Kahn and Wiener's data to propose that at least eighteen nations are already in the industrial stage judged by per capita income; and that another forty or fifty will reach the 'mature industrial' or 'mass consumption' stages by the end of the century.

These latter views all operationalise the concept of industrial society in economic and technological ways, but this represents only one part of the industrial society idea. It is the social consequences of such technologies that have interested the sociologist. Thus we find Cotgrove's survey of the field concluding that industrial society can be contrasted with 'traditional' society as having

experienced a demographic revolution with a sharp decline in both birth-rate and death rate, a decrease in the size, scope and pervasiveness of the family, an opening up of the stratification system with the shift from ascribed to achieved status, a levelling of culture with the development of mass communications and mass education, and the secularization and bureaucratization of society . . . The increasing division of labour which characterizes mechanization, and the organization of the labour force in factory production is normally accompanied by work relations which are functionally specific (confined to specified duties), impersonal, and affectively neutral (based on contractual relations rather than personal loyalties). (Cotgrove, 1967, pp. 271–2)

Underlying these changes is the central force of modern science, as most writers have emphasised.

Science and technology have made it possible for 3 billion human beings to live on this earth, for the standard of living to rise from year to year in advanced countries . . . The *qualitative* difference between present-day and earlier science and technology is *obviously* the indispensable pre-condition of all the other features usually attributed to modern societies: the lengthening of the life-span, the steady increase in national output, the predominant and at times obsessional concern with production and expansion, the creation of an artificial environment for human life, vast labour and administrative organizations, specialization, intellectual and social rationalization, etc. It would be easy to show that none of the phenomena that observers consider essential to modern society would be possible without the development of science and technology. (Aron, 1967 p. 99).

Although Aron is more explicit in his concentration on the role of science, he is not particularly exceptional. As Moore has concluded in his survey of theories of modernisation,

It is reasonably proper, though conventional, therefore, to consider modernization in terms of economic growth. In fact, we may pursue the convention further and speak of the process as *industrialization.* Industrialization means the extensive use of inanimate sources of power for economic production, and all that that entails by way of organization, transportation, communication, and so on . . . The studies of social change that take industrialization as a starting point are extremely numerous. (Moore, 1963, pp. 91–2)

He goes on to list much the same set of characteristics as Cotgrove, adding changes to the institutions of property, labour and the state which have resulted from industrialisation (seen as a technical process rather than in its more general sense of encompassing its associated social concomitants (1963, pp. 94–105).

A convenient summary of these processes is to be found in Kerr *et al.* (1973, p. 56). Under the heading of 'The Logic of Industrialisation' the authors offer a simple chart which is reproduced here as Table 3.1.

In stressing the characteristics of industrial society as a type, a weak form of convergence thesis is implicitly adopted. Kerr *et al.* are, of course, exponents of a much stronger form of this argument that societies tend to converge to one social and political order because of their common technology. Even if pre-existing conditions obscure the underlying pattern,

Table 3.1   The logic of industrialisation

Workforce	Increased skills and widening range of skills. Increasing occupational and geographic mobility. Higher levels of education more closely related to industrial function. Structured workforce.
Scale of society	Urbanisation and decline of agriculture as a way of life. Larger role for government.
Consensus in society	Increasing ideological consensus in a pluralistic society.
Worldwide industrialism	Industrial society spreads out from the centres of advanced technology.

the logic of industrialization prevails eventually ... Each industrialized society is more like every other industrialized society – however great the differences among them may be – than any industrial society is like any pre-industrial society. (Kerr *et al.* p. 283)

Other similar general statements can be found in Swanson (1971, pp. 137–8) and with an emphasis on class relations and organisations, in Scott (1979, pp. 17–18). An interesting comparison based on Parsons' pattern variables can be found in Banks (1964).

At risk of undoing this package so recently constructed, it must be said that there is no simple homogeneity of ideas underlying the summary. Aron (1967a) has attacked as superficial those accounts by statisticians and economists which rely on per capita income levels, proportions employed in non-agricultural industry, or percentages living in towns or receiving an education. Cotgrove (1967) observes that traditional forms of social organisation (e.g. labour and production) can coexist with modern forms. Kerr (1973) acknowledges that there are many different starting points and different roads for a society's journey through industrialisation. And Moore (Feldman and Moore, 1963) is critical of theories of social change which posit a series of crude evolutionary stages, which ignore the interaction of structural elements during industrialisation, and which assume that there is a final static stage of post-industrialisation as the end product of the industrialisation process (see respectively Aron, 1967a, pp. 54–5; Cotgrove, 1967, p. 272; Kerr, 1973, p. 298; and Feldman and Moore, 1963, p. 106).

Again, some of these accounts have been heavily ideological, reflecting the political climate of the Cold War, and particularly the McCarthy era of the 1950s. A concern for stable pluralist democracy is evident in the work of Rostow (1960), Kerr *et al.* (1973) and Lipset (1960). All three contain versions of industrial society which are heavily influenced by a US model, and as Aron has argued (following Vilar, Marcuse and others) even less political accounts also to some extent serve to 'camouflage capitalism by calling it industrial society' (Aron 1967b, pp. 94–5). This is because there is both a change in terminology, and a shift of focus from class relations and mode of production to the role of technology. Aron sees this for the most part as less an attempt at ideology than a genuine effort to encapsulate the unique spirit of Western societies, that is to say to come to terms with the importance of science for such societies. It is science that brings us that later variant of the basic theory, post-industrial society.

POST-INDUSTRIAL SOCIETY

It is not important for present purposes to dwell on the differences between 'industrial' and 'post-industrial' society. Both conceptions share the central concept of a science-based society, and despite differences of emphasis, there is a great deal of overlap. For example, Touraine's conception of post-industrial, 'technocratic', or 'pro-grammed' societies 'retains some characteristics of these earlier societies' (Touraine, 1974, p. 3), while Bell accepts that 'the post-industrial society is a continuation of trends unfolding out of industrial society' (Bell, 1974, p. 115). Indeed, Bell has some fun at the expense of scholars who, like himself, have adopted the prefix 'post' to identify contemporary developments (1974, pp. 51–8). While there may be some case for clarifying the two types of society for the sake of intellectual tidiness, it is of more interest to see how these later writers have *extended* earlier interpretations of twentieth-century society in the West.

The purpose of Touraine's nomenclature is not to suggest that in some magical way production and wealth have reached such levels that the post-industrial society can abandon concern with production and become a consumer and leisure society . . . The type of society we live in is more 'driven' by economic growth than any other. The individualized features of private life, as well as local societies and their ways of life have been profoundly affected – even destroyed – by ever-growing geographic and social mobility, by the massive diffusion of information and propaganda, and by broader political participation than ever before. Precisely these factors make it impossible for exclusively economic mechanisms to be maintained any longer at the centre of social organization and activity. (Touraine, 1974, p. 5)

It is the connection between production and knowledge, and the way in which this dominates the rest of society that prompts Touraine to talk about a 'programmed' society: 'All domains of social life – education, consumption, information, etc – are being more and more integrated into what used to be called production factors' (1974, p. 5). The new domination reduces man to an alienated state, where his entire life is conditioned by the ruling class: the new lines of class conflict therefore lie not between capital and labour, but between the structures of economic and political decision-making and those who are reduced to this 'dependent participation'.

By comparison, the position adopted by Bell (1974) is somewhat more 'optimistic', in that he sees the new groupings and their overriding concern with theoretical knowledge as providing a basis for a different kind of social integration and harmony. He identifies five 'dimensions' or 'components' of the term post-industrial society.

1. Economic sector: the change from a goods-producing to a service economy;
2. Occupational distribution: the pre-eminence of the professional and technical class;
3. Axial principle: the centrality of theoretical knowledge as the source of innovation and of policy formulation for the society;
4. Future orientation: the control of technology and technological assessment;
5. Decision-making: the creation of a new 'intellectual technology' (Bell, 1974, p. 14).

If this sounds much like the theorists of industrial society in the previous section, the distinctiveness of Bell's writing is that he argues his five dimensions are each much further advanced as tendencies than in industrial society, and that they will continue to become even more accentuated in the future.

Thus in the economic sector, developing the work of Clarke (1957) and Kuznets (1957), he distinguishes between the industrial society's expanding service sector – retailing, commerce, transport, communication and utilities – and the post-industrial services of health, education, research, and government. On the occupational dimension it is the growth not of skilled or technician labour, but that of the 'new intelligentsia' of scientists and technical experts, whose command of *theoretical* (as opposed to sophisticated empirical) knowledge requires at least a college education. In contrast to industrial society's development by haphazard technological innovation, post-industrial society is orientated towards planning and the coordination of change, while problem solving by means of rules-of-thumb or intuitive judgements is replaced by the application of systematic and complex rules, typified by computer algorithms. Although Bell sees the historical roots of these processes, he argues that for analytical purposes post-industrial society can be seen as a different type based on the cumulation of these elements. In industrial society

> the chief economic problem has been the problem of capital . . . the major social problem that of industrial conflict between employer and worker. To the extent that the investment process has been routinized and the 'class conflicts' encapsulated so that the issue of class strife no longer acts as to polarize a country around a single issue, those older problems of an industrial society have been muted if not 'solved'.
>
> In the post-industrial society, the chief problem is the organization of science, and the primary institution the university or the research institute. (Bell, 1974, p. 116)

The 'social problem' becomes one of control of decision-making, of bureaucratisation, and pluralistic competition in the political arena.

This image of a society in which knowledge and rationality reign supreme, despite the persuasiveness of Bell's argument, has attracted a number of critics. We have already noted in the previous chapter the arguments of Marglin and others to the effect that the kinds of technology developed and the rate of its introduction owe more to control (and profit) than to their efficiency. We might add, following Kumar (1976), that the 'war economy' of the 1950s and 1960s has done more to stimulate research (in terms of increasing its share of GNP) in America than any new interest in fundamental knowledge for its own sake. Post-war economic development has owed more to the further exploitation of existing knowledge than to original research. The idea that post-industrial society, increasingly influenced by the scientific and professional ethos, will follow a 'sociologizing' mode, concerned with non-market communal planning in the direction of maximum welfare. (Kumar, 1976, p. 352)

seems even more preposterous in Britain under the Thatcher administration than it did in the mid-1970s.

Nonetheless, Bell has identified, if exaggerated, an important aspect of post-industrial society in its economic and occupational shifts. Kumar seems to imply that major changes in the focus of economic activity (with increased planning and future orientation) and in the occupational structure, have no effect. But it has been axiomatic in mainstream sociology that a man's occupation relates to his whole social persona. That means that changes in occupational structure involve other social changes, so that Bell's analysis merits further consideration, not least in terms of occupational change and its effects. However, most of Bell's evidence – and there is a good deal of it – refers to US society, and it is not discussed here, although some parallel British evidence is reviewed in Chapter 6 below.

For convenience, we conclude this section on post-industrial society with Galbraith (1967) whose concept of a 'new industrial state' is another variation on the industrial/post-industrial theme. Galbraith's analysis includes the modern corporation in the set of characteristic features: large industrial organisations are at once *possible* because of technological production and national systems of administration, and also *promoters* of the values and the system which generate further technological advance and create employment for technical experts. With the economy dominated by very large and complex corporations, and capital drawn from numerous sources, the capitalist no longer controls his investment. Professional managers take his place, and with ever-increasing knowledge and specialisation, a new cadre of technical experts become indispensable to the corporation. This 'technostructure' 'extends from the leadership of the modern industrial enterprise down to just short of the labour force and embraces a large number of people and a large variety of talent' (Galbraith, 1967, p. 56). Their growth in number (and, paradoxically, their continued scarcity value) enables them to play an ever more influential role both in and outside of the corporation: their values are more liberal than those of the old style capitalists: a new industrial state replaces the old.

The parallels with Bell's new intelligentsia, and Touraine's techno-crats and bureaucrats, are obvious. Bell, it is true, attributes less to the role of modern capitalism as the cause of this change, while Touraine makes an important distinction between the upper echelons and the subsidiary level which is somewhat less clear in Galbraith's writing. But all three identify technology and the separation of ownership and control as having advanced to such a point that previous patterns of class relations no longer apply. If one wanted to force a distinction between post-industrial and industrial formulations, it would have to be that the latter have been more concerned with marking off modern society from pre-industrial forms, with the use of inanimate power, and with the nature of urbanism, affluence, and large-scale organisations. However, for present purposes this is unimportant, and for the remainder of this chapter the term 'industrial society' is used to include its post-industrial variants. This is permissible, if only because the various contributions share a similar style of exposition, many of the same intellectual themes, and say very much the same things about occupations.

OCCUPATIONAL CHANGE

We also propose to use the term 'occupational transition' to identify the kind of occupational change – i.e. the expansion of jobs requiring technical expertise – associated with the development of industrial society. The derivation is from 'demographic transition', the changes in demographic profiles which are also associated with industrialisation. Occupational transition is a convenient way of specifying particular changes: it is not a *theory* which explains those changes, nor is it a precise *statement* about the *scale* of those changes. The sociological significance of occupational transition, as against   form it takes, is logically a secondary question, and one which is taken up later. Here we are first concerned to see in more detail what kinds of occupational transition are generally said to occur.[1] Despite at least one argument to the contrary (see Jones, 1977), it is possible to identify a core of assumptions about the forms that occupational structures take in modern society as a result of the industrialisation process.

One of the most useful sources in this respect is W. E. Moore's *Social Change* (1974). Despite being a relatively small book (in both its 1963 and its revised 1974 editions) it has been fairly influential, not least because its brevity, coverage and precision have made it a popular undergraduate text, particularly in the USA. These same qualities explain its role here as representing a central tendency among other writers on the theory of industrial society. As Moore writes in the preface, the revised edition was designed to be

> selectively attentive both to the critical comments that have appeared in the sociological literature, and to the new approaches that have appeared here and there. Yet . . . I see little that adds to our precise and general knowledge of patterned sequences. (1974, pp. ix–x)

With this in mind, he has omitted descriptive studies in search of his prime goal of compact, dense exposition (1974, p. x).

From the wider range of Moore's work, it is possible to draw eight detailed propositions about occupational transition (1974, pp. 104–6). One of these – that there will be increased mobility both within careers and between generations – is left for discussion in Chapter 7 below. Three of the others can be regarded as general propositions:

1. All economic operations, such as the subsistence agriculture sector, are incorporated in the national market economy.
2. There is a change of economic activity from primary to secondary, and secondary to tertiary, industrial sectors.
3. New occupations are created, and differentiation between occupations increases.

The remaining four propositions deal more specifically with occupations.

4. The proportion of workers in agriculture will decline.
5. An upgrading of minimum and average skill levels will take place, resulting in a structure with relatively few unskilled workers and 'the vast majority' of workers in various middle categories.
6. There will, nonetheless, be a shortage of skilled workers.
7. This will be accompanied by an increase in demand for professionals of all categories, and in particular doctors, engineers and experts in organisation.

These propositions apply to countries both during industrialisation and in contemporary industrial economies (Moore, 1974, pp. 104–5).

Moore is not alone in adopting this view of occupational change, although in contrast other writers have been less succinct (Kerr *et al.*'s (1973) work is less easy to abbreviate into a brief coherent statement!). The same basic approach can be seen in a variety of writers: Appelbaum's (1971) account closely resembles that of Moore, but with greater emphasis on convergence (pp. 45–50). Weinberg (1969) has commented that 'there are implicit criteria of convergence in many discussions of industrialisation' (p. 4). Aron (1976b) says that

> all industrial societies have similar characteristics from this point of view. The proportion of intellectual or semi-intellectual occupations inevitably increases in industrial society. More and more supervisors, engineers and people with technical qualifications are needed. Everybody must be able to read and write. Thus two of the occupational categories become larger and larger, the technical intelligentsia who direct the industrial workers and the non-technical intelligentsia, or those whose technical qualifications are mainly literary. (Aron, 1967b, pp. 23–4)

Galbraith, Bell, and Touraine, as we have seen above, and Crosland (1956), Hoselitz (1954) and Trieman (1970) are other examples, while Kerr in particular stresses the technological imperative: 'the same industries in different countries use roughly similar technologies with roughly similar proportions of workers in jobs of varying skill and wage levels' (Kerr, 1973, p. 248). Even Kerr's critics have largely operated within his framework of assumptions about the occupational structure of industrial society: among the contributors to the well-known *Sociological Review Monograph* edited by Halmos, only Platt addresses herself directly to this question (Platt, 1964). This is because the critical contributions, including those of Lockwood, Goldthorpe, Banks, Worsley and Marshall, were concerned with the *consequences for stratification theory* of the changes in occupations, or with the *dynamic force behind* such changes. They were not concerned with the actual changes themselves. As Garnsey (1975) observed of this collection of writings

> while the predominance of the economic and technological factors in determining the distribution of rewards and opportunities in industrial societies has been disputed, the notion that 'the structural and functional pre-requisites of a developing technology and economy result in the occupational distributions of advanced societies being patterned in a fairly standardised way' has not been seriously called into question. Goldthorpe was concerned rather with the corollary of this thesis . . . [he] does not actually challenge the notion that in its main features a certain occupational structure is an invariable and inherent feature of industrialization. (Garnsey, 1975, pp. 439–40)

Indeed, it is almost impossible to read an account of social change written in the 1960s and early 1970s without encountering this basic assumption about occupational transition. It was particularly influential in work on education and social mobility, where it was central to the work of Glass (1954, p. 24), Floud and Halsay (1958, pp. 169–70 and 1961, pp. 1–2), and Little and Westergaard (1964, p. 302). However, there has been until recently relatively little active investigation of the form of changes that have been assumed to take place. Clearly a necessary step to be undertaken is to investigate further the precise nature of occupational transition (Payne, 1977a, and 1977b; and Kendrick *et al.*, 1982). Such an analysis would need to examine how different theories of industrial society have proposed various forms of occupational transition. Touraine's distinction between technocrats and bureaucrats, for example, is less concerned with the middle of the occupational hierarchy, while Bell's 'new intelligentsia' stresses the top, and Galbraith's technostructure model covers a much wider field. Within the considerable limits of available data, it would be desirable to show how far these versions of occupational transition have become part of our understanding of the framework in which mobility takes place.

Bell is somewhat more explicit on occupational transition than others, linking it firmly to sectoral shift between industries in line with his concentration on knowledge rather than technology.

> The spread of services, particularly in trade, finance, education, health, and government, conjures up the picture of a white-collar society. But all services are not white-collar, since they include transportation workers and auto repairmen. But then, not all manufacturing is blue-collar work. In 1970 the white-collar component within manufacturing – professional, managerial, clerical, and sales – came to almost 31 per cent of that work force. The change-over to a post-industrial society is signified not only by the change in sector distribution – the place *where* people work – but in the pattern of occupations, the *kind* of work they do. (Bell, 1974, pp. 133–4)

Bell argues that the 'dramatic' change in proportions of white-collar workers is 'somewhat deceptive' because most white-collar workers have been women and 'in American Society, as in most others, family status is still evaluated on the basis of the man's job' (1974, p. 134). It is therefore only the change to *men's* occupations that is significant.

This seems a dubious kind of argument. Even if we accept that men and women work for different reasons, that work has a different meaning for them, and that they are employed in different jobs, this is an argument for analysing them separately, but not for ignoring female employment (Bell deals with female labour in a single page, under a section headed 'Some Labour Problems of the Post Industrial Society' (1974, p. 145)). It is the expansion of white-collar work that is the characteristic of industrial society, *not* the gender of those who fill the new occupational niches. That is a secondary problem. Perhaps it is a further and as yet neglected characteristic of industrial society that a higher proportion of its jobs are done by women and that a higher proportion of women are engaged in waged work. This in turn poses the question of why it is the less prestigious jobs which go to women: is this an inherent feature of industrial society, or just a transitional pattern of adjustment? Again, if the female labour force is mobilised into the market, how does this affect the chances of a male in seeking employment? And does the status of while-collar work, or the husband-based US family status system, remain unchanged? It is implicit in Bell's work that when more *men* do white-collar work *it matters*: why else does he dwell on the growth and role of the 'new intelligentsia'?

The present author does not pretend to have the answers to all of these questions, although some further discussion of them can be found elsewhere (Payne *et al.*, 1983). The most immediate of those issues for an analysis of social mobility is how should the opportunity structure for men be conceptualised?

While it is true that women tend to be concentrated into separate occupational categories from men (see Hakim, 1979; Payne *et al.*, 1980), if one is to argue that changes in demand for labour generate new mobility flows, then on the face of it men and women are both potential candidates. Given the relative separation of their spheres of employment, we must modify that initial statement to say that the rules of female employment in general operate to insulate the male labour force from potential female competition. By rules we mean not just hiring or promotion procedures, but domestic constraints, socialisation, public attitudes, etc.: the whole gamut of processes which have been analysed by feminist sociologists in the last decade. By insulate, we do not mean that women never compete for the same jobs but that only a small part of the potential female labour force attempt (or are allowed to attempt) to compete for certain jobs: this leaves the field more or less free for the men. Clearly an attempt to reconceptualise the logic of industrialism in terms of gender is long overdue.

EXTRA-OCCUPATIONAL DEVELOPMENTS

This is relevant to one of the more recent views of modern society, namely that of Gershuny (1978). He has argued that post-industrial society is a self-service economy, in which what was previously production activity has become consumption activity in the domestic (and therefore to a degree, female) sphere.

> There are grounds for suggesting that future provision of services in developed countries may be increasingly extra-economic, that jobs in service industries may be replaced by activities undertaken within households or by other sorts of voluntary associations outside the money economy . . . people no longer *buy* the final service from railway or bus systems, but instead *buy* cars, and *produce the final service themselves.* (Gershuny 1978, p. 134, original emphasis)

A similar argument is made for replacing servants by consumer durables, and the trend to 'in-home' entertainments. Gershuny distinguishes 'final service', i.e. direct provision, from 'indirect service', such as the production of a service good. The more that consumers carry out this final service themselves, the fewer jobs that are created in service industry. Indeed, because consumer products are essential to a self-service economy, a proportion of new jobs are created in *manufacturing* industry, not the tertiary sector. Indeed one might observe that the new manufacturing jobs are not necessarily located in the same society: jobs can be 'exported' to Third World countries (Fröbel *et al.*, 1980) so that the net result is unemployment in the service society itself.

Gershuny does not, however, reject the thesis of skills enhancement. He contrasts the idea of a service economy (what here has been called industrial or post-industrial society) with its undifferentiated drift towards tertiary industry and tertiary occupations, with his conception of a self-service economy, where, 'because of automation and divison of labour, a trend towards more white-collar employment is combined with a progressive concentration of employment in manufacturing industry' (Gershuny, 1978, p. 146). This formal economy coexists with an informal economy in which leisure services are produced and consumed.

In his later work, Gershuny has shifted the emphasis of his argument away from a growth in manufacturing employment towards a more sophisticated model of occupational transition in which the most important outcome is the growth of 'administrative, professional and technical workers, mainly located in the service section (Gershuny,

1983, p. 96). He combines five elements into a revised sequence of sectoral shift: the demand for 'luxury' services; 'social innovation' (the consumer/Do-it-yourself argument); subcontracting from manufacturing to service industry; the 'productivity gap' between high productivity in manufacturing and lower productivity in the services; and 'occupational tertiarisation' which reduces the proportion of manual workers in all industries (Gershuny and Miles, 1983, pp. 249–50). The driving forces in this more specified model are both the social innovation process (closely related to 'demand' expressed in consumer choice) and technological innovation, which operates at variable rates. He thus offers an argument in which changes in demand operate on production, and changes in production operate on consumption and employment (Gershuny, 1983, pp. 1–2).

In his discussion of occupations Gershuny alerts us to several key changes:

> employment has tended to grow rather rapidly (albeit from fairly small bases) in producer services whose service products form intermediate inputs into other industries (examples include many financial, communications, and business services). Employment growth has also been rapid in non-marketed final services, typically involving state institutions . . . For many marketed final services (for example, transport and entertainment) however, there has been something of a decline. (Gershuny and Miles, 1983, p. 4)

For the last two decades, his European data show broadly similar rates of change, with the 'occupational effect outweighing the sectoral effects by more than two to one . . . occupational employment in the economy as a whole is more affected by technical and organizational change in production processes than by change in the pattern of demand' (Gershuny, 1983, p. 109 and Appendix 7).

Much of the evidence which Gershuny presents fits quite well with the author's own empirical work (albeit with broad categories), which makes his work attractive. With regard to a theory of mobility grounded in industrial society, his argument points towards the need to examine sectors and periods of change at a more detailed level than earlier studies, not least the tertiary sector which holds the key to occupational transition. Such detailed work can at times be tedious and will often be frustrated by a lack of comparability between, or even availability of, data. However, Gershuny poses a further problem of estimating the importance of social innovation in contemporary society. Such a self-service or informal economy involves more kinds of extra-economic, or more strictly extra-occupational, activity. Production of services in a non-waged way removes those activities, or even the people producing services, from the occupational realm, so that mobility conceived in occupational terms cannot encompass them (as is presently the case of women in unwaged work).

A similar view of the division of labour has been recently advocated by Pahl (1984). His study of the Isle of Sheppey, together with historical materials, makes a plausible case for reconceptualising work. This would shift occupation from centre stage, to allow for the many 'self-provisioning' activities that may be counted as work, but which do not form part of regular, standardised, paid employment. While Pahl offers a rounding-out of our picture of work which helps to conceptualise domestic labour, and balances an otherwise one-dimensional view, it would be wrong to lay too much emphasis on the informal economy if it obstructed an analysis of paid employment. Social mobility as yet cannot cope with occupations, let alone with the para-occupational world. It is still the case that occupation is important, even if it is not all-inclusive. Self-services require income from paid employment in order to purchase materials and equipment (Pahl, 1984, p. 317).

Nor do Gershuny and Pahl fully explain the relationship between stratification perceived as occupation based and these informal activities. Gershuny offers virtually no comment on this subject. Pahl is aware of this difficulty, although he is more concerned first to construct his new perspective, rather than develop connections between an older model of class and the non-occupational economic activities. He argues that Marxist accounts of class and social integration fail to recognise the lack of articulation between class and status, because, 'Marx and the other political economists focussed on only *some* of the work of *some* of the workers' (Pahl, 1984, p. 88, original emphasis).

The consciousness of social actors is not totally determined either by the class relations of the work place, nor are those class relations typically those of manual workers. It follows from this (a position drawing on Lockwood) that a social mobility which uses occupation to express movements between classes is equally limited in what it can offer about social integration. However, a mobility based on occupation, being less ambitious, deals with that part of the picture which is attributable to full-time paid employment. It is thus limited, but less flawed.

This does not resolve the problem of balancing between the occupational and the extra-occupational. Although both Pahl and Gershuny are convincing within the discussion of their chosen cases, how central are these examples to daily life? This is a criticism which applies to both, but in particular to Gershuny. In the first place, the types of self-service (or self-provisioning) may be important, but the examples presented – various forms of domestic labour, home videos, private cars – are few in number. But there are many other services which already can be done in the home but are only done so by a very small minority. For example, home brewing and home food production, house conveyancing, parental education, clothes making, are all activities which could be much more developed in the informal economy than they presently are. Each offers the equal potential for the substitution of a sale of products which can be used in self-service, for the provision of a service (or as Gershuny argues as his dynamic, the substitution of *profit* from sale, for *cost* of a salary of the service worker). Against the potential for self-service, domestic labour (effectively dying out by the 1920s), the rise of private motoring (a phenomenon of the 1950s and 1960s) and the boom in home entertainments (still a minority sport even in the 1980s) seem curiously sparse and historically spaced.

This really is not too surprising once one recognises how much of the tertiary sector is not amenable to self-provision (the distinction between final service and other levels is not important for the present analysis). It is not easy to see how the operations of the public sector, as against the private, could be diversified. Do-it-yourself town and country planning, independent nuclear weapons systems, and domestic taxation are non-starters, not to mention most health and education. And even many of the 'private' services, once we exclude transport and possibly construction, are not susceptible to informalisation except for very limited parts of the population: telecommunications, banking, insurance and commerce are examples where the service is provided more for organisations than for individuals or families. It is in these areas that new occupations are being invented.

Gershuny can be seen, therefore, to overestimate the importance of the phenomenon he identifies. Nonetheless, his observations serve to make several points. Clearly, technology does not *necessarily* create new jobs, particularly in the service sector. It *may* do so, but that remains an empirical question. Second, his data are a reminder that occupational change is not confined to the tertiary sector: occupational upgrading occurs in manufacturing too. Finally, his analysis shows how within a broad sector, different forces may be at work so that a separation of, say old staples from newer manufacturing industries, or transport from other service activity may well reveal distinctive modes of mobility. In other words, conventional industry sector analysis may need to be expanded.

RECENT SECTORAL MOVEMENTS

This is further confirmation of the view already expressed in this chapter. Bell's (1974) own evidence shows that sectoral shift is only a rough guide to occupational distribution. Is it therefore worth considering sectors at all? For Bell, the answer is, of course, 'yes', because he is interested in *all* characteristics of industrialism, and the growth of the tertiary sector (transport and utilities), the quarternary sector (trade, finance, insurance, real estate) and the quinary sector (health, education, research, government and recreation) are used to show how the resources of a post-industrialising society are increasingly devoted to knowledge-based industries. For Bell, and more so for other writers like Touraine, Galbraith, and Dahrendorf, the emergence of a new class on the basis of their 'knowledge resources' is predicted on the existence of institutions of employment to hire the members of the new class. But how far is this relevant to the more traditional area of mobility and stratification?

If we leave on one side the underlying rationale that we require a general explanatory framework to account for occupational transition, there are two important points arising from sectoral analysis. The first (and it is one that could also be drawn from the theory of capitalist society) is that technological change creates new occupations, and therefore that *mobility will be greatest where there has been most technological change.* 'Technology' in this context is used to encompass 'social technology' as well as purely physical technology. Second, there will be more mobility in the quarternary and quinary sectors (although there is no need to insist on those distinctions) than in the primary and secondary sectors. However, following Gershuny and Bell's point about white-collar work in manufacturing industry, there will be more mobility in 'high tech' production industries than in other more traditional parts of the secondary sector. Third, mobility will be most evident at those historical times when there is greatest or most rapid technological innovation.

The first and second of these propositions are much easier to test empirically than the third. The third requires detailed knowledge of the history of many different industries, and given the other two propositions, the effect of the third may be harder to identify. Again, current events tend to suggest that technical innovation leads to a reduced labour force, as those with obsolete skills are discarded.

Rothwell and Zegveld (1979) have recently implied that the era of major sectoral shift may be passed. Citing the reaction against government spending in the USA and counter-inflationary policies in Europe, they argue that the public sector service industries of education, environmental services and welfare cannot continue to expand because of the reduction in public finances,

> the main hopes for future service employment growth must lie in the expansion of the private sector, and if aggregate demand is raised sufficiently, then this must surely exert a demand for goods and services somewhere in the economic system with a growth in jobs to provide these extra goods and services. (Rothwell and Zegveld, 1979, p. 48)

Even so, they go on to suggest that the response in manufacturing industry may well be one of increased production without any comparable increase in employment, as the technology of labour-saving equipment is now so well established. They use the term 'jobless growth' to identify a period which begins in the 1960s and is clearly present by the 1970s, since when most OECD countries have experienced an absolute decline in employment in manufacturing.

The difference between employment and productivity is also emphasised by Browning and Singelmann (whose 1978 work in fact is more in the tradition outlined in the previous chapter). They argue that both primary and secondary sectors in the USA have been characterised by marked increases in output but absolute and relative declines in employment in agriculture. Goods-producing is more susceptible to technological inputs designed to increase productivity than services, because non-material products are harder to standardise. Increasing productivity in agriculture and manufacturing 'allows for economic growth and rising national and per capita income, which in turn stimulates a rising demand for various kinds of services' (Browning and Singelmann 1978, p. 485). They conclude that, as far as the USA is concerned, 'the most dynamic phase' of sectoral transformation should have occurred by 1970, leaving little relative change in proportions of employment between sectors in the rest of the century. The transfer of employment between industries is almost complete, a conclusion recently confirmed in a paper by Singelmann (1985). Gershuny's somewhat cruder data for several European countries, on the other hand, suggest continued shifts (Gershuny and Miles 1983, Appendix 4).

Browning and Singelmann also propose an elaboration of the primary/secondary/tertiary model, in which the tertiary sector is replaced by four separate sectors: distributive services; producer services (i.e. commerce); social services (welfare and public administration); and personal services (entertainment and personal consumption). They report a similarity to the typologies independently derived by Katouzian and Singer (Browning and Singelmann, 1978, p. 491; Katouzian, 1970; Singer, 1971). The common element is that a distinction is made between industry or production oriented services (distributive and producer services); services which are collectively consumed and provided directly or indirectly by the state, such as health and educational and personal or individual services which relate to leisure consumption.

What this section has shown is that the basic idea of technological change leads to a variety of rather more sophisticated positions. In particular, the complexity of the processes involved poses a problem for the present study, because if mobility is dependent on patterns of employment, then these patterns of employment are changing in a number of different ways. While an analysis based on the major sectors of primary, secondary, and tertiary industry is obviously improvement on earlier levels, it is theoretically, if not always pragmatically, possible to explore even more detailed subdivisions of economic activity.

Given that the creation of new occupations is focused in some sectors and not others, and in some times, and not others, and that mobility may be similarly concentrated, then changes in the class structure must be similarly differentially located within society. It follows that, while an aggregated account of mobility is useful, the basic approach of grounding it will call for disaggregation. This in turn must tend to shift the emphasis away from monolithic classes, and towards a multifaceted model, in which there are many social situations, which in turn generate complex status identities and relations. As we shall see in the next chapter, even those writers in the post-industrial society school have a great deal to say about the kinds of social information and integration which arise as a consequence of having advanced technologies as an integral element in society.

5 Class and Labour Markets in Contemporary Society

Although the previous chapter dealt with industrial society as a type, the discussion inevitably involved ideas about occupational structure and class. If industrial society is based on the separation of ownership and control, and the growth of knowledge (processes also exercising theorists of capitalist society) then the basis for social formation changes. A number of writers, most notably Touraine, Parkin, Giddens, Dahrendorf, and Goldthorpe, have suggested ways in which the new occupational roles provide the basis for new classes.

In keeping with the importance of science in such a society, Touraine's new ruling class consists not of capitalists, but of high level technocrats. 'Technocrats are not technicians but managers, whether they belong to the administration of the State or to big businesses' (1974, pp. 49–50). Nor are they a unitary group: some favour capital accumulation, while others propagate public consumption, and alliances continually shift. Membership is defined by

> knowledge and a certain level of education . . . the education of the top level tends to be independent of our specialized body of professors and is largely provided for by members of the elite . . . A hierarchical continuity among bureaucrats [middle management] and technocrats may appear to exist but it is a rare case when the members of a great organisation cannot recognize the line that separates them. (Touraine, 1974, pp. 51–2)

The technocrats may suffer gains or losses over time, but they do not lose their position, either individually or as a group. Secure in their jobs and income, a social group is formed which while not being homogeneous, nevertheless develops a degree of self-consciousness, a distinctive life-style, and which 'exercises considerable control over recruitment' (1974, p. 53).

Beneath them the bureaucrats operate the elaborated systems of communication and control which are necessary for the operation of a planned, technological economy – and society. They are not a 'service

71

class' in Renner's meaning: functionaries without any discretion operating a bureaucracy in a narrow Weberian sense. These bureaucrats are

> adept at change, agents of progress beyond doubt, but also often careerists, vain, distrustful, absorbed in their subtle stratagems and their desire to re-inforce their own importance by holding back information, by fostering their own prestige in every way possible, and by defending the internal demands of the organization in opposition to its external purposes. (1974, p. 58).

'Professionals', particularly in higher education and health, are the marginal category, while 'experts' like engineers, accountants, lawyers, psychologists, GPs and teachers are on a par with the bureaucrats (1974, pp. 64–6).

Besides them, and in Touraine's eyes, contrasted to them are the technicians: technical workers, designers, higher ranking office workers, excluded from and resenting the bureaucratic game, weak in authority, influence or negotiating power, and different from the proletariat only in that their jobs are less repetitive, monotonous, and restrictive.

This way of representing Touraine's idea emphasises the elements of occupation and class, and plays down his analysis of the student movement, and the cultural and political life of France in the 1960s, for obvious reasons. As well as being more relevant to our main theme of mobility and stratification, it serves as a corrective to any tendency to see the theory of industrial society as merely an ideological tool, concerned only with consensus, affluence, and rationality. While Touraine rejects sociological analysis based on the idea of two basic classes, or on the interplay of the traditional production processes, land, labour and capital, he also rejects the suggestion 'that advanced industrial societies no longer have class structures' (1974, pp. 81–2). His analysis shows how the occupational character of a science-based economy changes the nature of class conflict, both by rewarding class boundaries and by shifting the locus of the conflict. It is true, as Kumar (1976) has observed, that Touraine does not elaborate on all aspects of his view of class, such as the proposal that the educated class is internally divided, but the notion of conflict is part and parcel of his analysis.

Parkin (1979) argues that industrial society is not dominated by the social relations of the capitalist firm. On the one hand the state is a major employer, while on the other (following Dahrendorf) work relationships do not dominate all other non-work activities. Thus while work is justifiably a major focus of interest, non-Marxist sociology, concerned with the division of labour 'as the main area in which observable realities of class played themselves out' (1979, p. 14), has defined out of existence 'the sister concept of capital' and yet at the same time failed to recognise the salience of other sources of social differentiation. Race, religion, language and gender are all independent bases for cleavage or coherence: 'A model of class relations that addresses itself exclusively to inequalities surrounding the occupational order is therefore bound to be defective' (1979, p. 15). Parkin uses the concept of closure to demonstrate how groups may restrict access to resources and opportunity: in 'modern capitalist society' closure takes two main forms, those institutions relating to property, and academic or professional qualifications. It is the latter that most concerns the present analysis.

Parkin identifies several groups within the middle class who have established control over entry to their occupations, based on possession of educational credentials (this being a viable strategy because of the technical nature of work tasks in industrial society). Here, closure is on occupational lines: class and occupation coincide. Their shared identity comes from their strategy of closure, not from property ownership nor from any 'indispensibility' of their function. However, the credentialist closure has a drawback: it makes transmission of socially-advantaged occupational positions to one's own children much more difficult:

> Dense children of the professional middle class . . . will continue to stumble at the intellectual assault course set up largely for their *parents*' own protection. Conversely, large numbers of bright children of the culturally dispossessed will sail through to claim the prize of professional entry. (Parkin, 1979, p. 61, original emphasis)

Parkin regards the middle class as having been 'guilty of grevous errors and miscalculations in its reproductive designs' (1979, p. 62) to allow so much upward and downward mobility. Even if the examination system does work in favour of the expensively schooled or otherwise socially advantaged, so reducing the risk of competition from the offspring of other classes, the patterns of mobility can only be explained by a misguided commitment to credentialism as a system based on sponsorship and careful selection, rather than hereditary transmission.

However, there are several alternative views that we can advance to a model of self-inflicted injury. First, while the professional middle class may be extremely powerful, that is not to say that as a class it is all-powerful. There is no need to believe that any one class exerts anything like total control over social events. Second, the expansion of new professions outpaces the credentialist procedure: new professions take time to impose closure, while demand for expertise in the short run exceeds supply. Third, again as we shall see, the process of credential competition in fact becomes important only in the 1960s, at which point some indices of upward mobility begin to suggest that the middle class starts to achieve higher rates of self-recruitment.

Parkin's account of credentialism and mobility shares some similarities with that of Giddens (1973) not least because of a common debt to Weber's ideas on non-class sources of association. Giddens also identifies possession of educational or technical qualifications as one of his three sorts of market capacity, arguing that within the non-manual middle class,

> the most significant type of difference in market capacity is undoubtedly between the capacity to offer marketable technical knowledge, recognised and specialised symbolic skills, and the offering of general symbolic competence. (Giddens, 1973, p. 186)

Professional credentials are what mark off draughtsmen and social workers from routine white-collar workers, not their place in the hierarchy of organisations or as a bridge between rulers and ruled. Qualifications, together with possession of property and manual labour power 'tend to be tied to closed patterns of inter- and intra-generation mobility' to yield a three-class core system (1973, p. 107).

Giddens sees mobility as playing a key role in linking market capacity to the formation of socially identifiable classes. This

> mediate structuration of class relationships is governed above all by the distribution of mobility chances which pertain within a given society . . . the greater the degree of 'closure' of mobility chances – both intergenerationally and within the career of the individual – the more this facilitates the formation of identifiable classes. (1973, p. 107)

However, Giddens is theorising on the basis of the 1949 Glass study of mobility (and possibly on a misreading of Miller's (1960) comparative data),

> virtually all movement, whether upward or downward, inter- or intragenerational, across the non-manual/manual division is 'short-range': that is to say, takes place in such a way as to minimise achieved differences in market capacity. (Giddens, 1973, p. 181).

He also assumes more or less constant rates of mobility (1973, p. 182). As will be shown on page 123 (and as the results of the Nuffield Study also show) there is in fact considerable 'long-range' mobility, and mobility rates do vary. Therefore the formation of socially identifiable classes is a *weaker* process than Giddens implies, because there is less closure of mobility.

Although on the surface he is dealing with class structuration and classes, Giddens, like Parkin, necessarily places occupation very much to the fore, because occupations are a kind of concrete representation of market capacity; qualifications and mobility processes relate to entry to occupations. Similarly in identifying the manual working class, he uses the division of labour in the sense of 'the allocation of occupational tasks within the productive organisation' (Giddens, 1973, p. 108). In other words, Giddens draws on those key attributes of industrial society, the technical division of labour and the importance of knowledge, to identify class formation. Of course, he links these ideas to others, such as ownership of property, and 'distinctive groupings', so that class formation is a more dynamic, complex, and less technologically determined process than in, say the writing of the convergence theorists. Nonetheless, his formulation depends on many of the same basic understandings about the social relations of technology in industrial society, while the emphasis placed on mobility provides an important link between occupations and classes.

Parkin and Giddens share with Dahrendorf (1959) the view that contemporary society is no longer to be explained primarily by the ownership of the means of production, but the latter differs markedly in where he places the emphasis. The sheer scale of activities outside of the capitalist–employee relationships – as much in bureaucratised firms as in the state apparatus – indicates a social order in which classes far from being missing, own their existence to forces beyond property. Dahrendorf identifies authority relations as the key, rather than the market situation (1959, pp. 136–40), rejecting occupation and market situation *per se* as bases for classes. The authority structure becomes 'the structural determinant of class formation and class conflict' (1959, p. 136). More recently, Dahrendorf has presented his view of a fragmented middle class with a heavy emphasis on access to educational qualifications (1982, pp. 57–9).

Goldthorpe's position lies between these two views. His use of the term 'service class' expresses the idea of property-based authority positions, but his framework is firmly based in market and work situations. For the service class to be

a class of employees who are appointed to the positions they hold, some higher agency is evidently presupposed . . . [having] power, whether the bases of this are economic, political, military or whatever. (Goldthorpe, 1982, p. 170)

The members of the service class are

> typically engaged in the exercise of delegated authority or in the application of specialist knowledge and expertise, operate in their work tasks and roles with a distinctive degree of autonomy and discretion . . . [and] are accorded conditions of employment which are also distinctive in both the level and kinds of rewards that are involved. In other words, professional, administrative and managerial employees are in these ways typically differentiated from other grades of employee – and most obviously wage-workers – in the character of both their work and market situations. (1982, p. 169)

Goldthorpe differs from Giddens in seeing that these shared elements justify the treatment of managers and professionals as occupying a single class location, even if their precise technical function is not identical.

Both of the above quotations also show how dependent Goldthorpe is on employment even when dealing directly with conceptions of social class. His position *vis-à-vis* industrial society is, however, a sophisticated one. The growth of professional and managerial occupations is presented as 'response to organisational exigencies' and being possible because of 'economic growth'. Nonetheless, this is *not* taken to mean that the growth is a 'natural' development of the division of labour in the course of 'economic growth' as sectoral shift accounts (e.g. Clarke, 1957) imply. Rather the service class's form reflects 'the structures of organisational and political power and the character of dominant values and ideologies' (Goldthorpe, 1982, pp. 302–3). By implication (although it is not very evident from his main work on mobility) Goldthorpe sets class formation in discrete historical and social settings, so marking himself off from many of the main theorists of industrial society whose accounts have suffered from both a lack of case studies and an uncertainty about the connections between the elements in economic change that they sought to theorise.

MOBILITY AND LABOUR MARKETS

Because mobility research has been inspired by an interest in class structures, it has taken as its unit of analysis either whole social structures (i.e. societies) or, for reasons of practicality, geographically discrete settlements like cities. The individual is seen as competing against all other individuals within that unit to achieve the 'best' occupation possible. Individuals are not equal, so that the outcome of the competition reflects the handicaps (family origin, qualifications, etc.) of the competitors. This process resembles the operation of a labour market, and in particular its implicit assumptions closely resemble those of neo-classical economics.

However, the significance of this has not previously been recognised, because mobility research has not generally taken its occupational dimension sufficiently seriously. However, Kaufman *et al.* (1981, p. 1) list several 'students of stratification (who) have begun exploring structural characteristics of jobs, firms and industries', while Smith (1983) explores mobility and labour markets for football coaches (see also Kreckel, 1980). The connection between mobility, labour markets and ideas of class is taken up in the final section of this chapter.

There are several components to the idea of a labour market: the rules which operate to cost labour, and regulate employment, as well as the mechanisms which allocate labour to jobs and control skill acquisition. Neo-classical economics treats labour in the same way as other commodities in positing a single, perfectly competitive market. The normal laws of supply and demand apply, with the worker (as supplier of labour) maximising his rewards in a rational manner by adjusting his wage demands and his geographical location in response to those laws. In a more sophisticated version, the market may be regarded as disaggregated into different skill levels, but the same principles then apply within these sectors. On the supply side, rational economic man is assumed to have the knowledge which enables him to evaluate all opportunities and to decide which balance of costs and benefits best suits him: the worker exercises choice. On the demand side, the employer is interested in the productive potential of labour as against alternative factors of production, and therefore differentiates between workers as units of labour according to their qualifications, experience, work record, etc. He sets up a hierarchy of utility, which manifests itself in wage differentials, rewarding most those workers with the greatest productive potential. In exercising his choice of whom he will employ, he seeks to constrain the choice available to the worker.

The similarities of this to the unspoken assumptions of mobility analysis are evident. Distribution to destinations comes about through inter-individual competition, with the interaction between the supply of individuals having particular attributes, and the demand of occupational opportunities having certain entry requirements, representing the framework in which that competition takes place. The handicaps of origin which explain the outcome for any given set of individuals are those already implied: the rules of employment, the acquisition of skills, the means by which workers are distributed among jobs. The central conception of mobility echoes perfect competition in that it measures deviation of the observed pattern from the expectation under perfect mobility. Apart from providing an economic, as opposed to a sociological, principle as the core explanatory device and dealing more explicitly with the demand side of the relationship, the neo-classical economic formulation of the labour market takes the same underlying model as social mobility analysis.

There are therefore two sufficient reasons why a discussion of mobility requires some consideration of labour market theory. First, the logic of taking mobility's occupational dimension seriously must immediately establish a connection with areas of sociology previously compartmentalised under the heading of 'work' rather than 'mobility'. Second, the congruence of the underlying models suggests that labour market theory is one of the more fruitful of these areas to explore, not least because it points to assumptions in mobility research which have hitherto received little attention. In particular, recent criticisms of orthodox labour market theory hold out the promise of generating parallel critiques of mobility theory. What we are working towards at this point is a reformulation of the social mobility process as a labour market process.

In the first place, although it can be assumed that all workers require employment, the labour force is not in a constant state of flux, with every member actively seeking to change his employment at the same instant. Eighty per cent to 90 per cent of people are in work, and remain in the same post for some time. Anything less than this would render conventional economic activity impossible, because of the high turnover of personnel in any one institution: the case of an office dependent on the services of 'temps' is a good example of how, without a stable work force, efficient operation is severely impaired. Low labour turnover is in the interest of the employer, as it ensures continuity of procedures. It is also frequently in the interests of employees, who avoid the upheaval of frequent changes both in their work routines and in those of work colleagues. Even if we assume that labour inertia reflects a conscious maximisation strategy on the part of the workers, it still means that the active workings of the market are confined to a marginal process. Everyone must at some stage seek employment, but at any one time, the market is likely to be relatively inactive.

But how do those who are seeking employment make their choices? In the first place, the 'choice' of employment is seen as not following strictly rational, optimising behaviour. This may not seem very significant to a sociological audience, but the more recent contributions to labour market theory are part of dialogue with neo-classical economics, in which, for example, rational economic man has a central place. As Loveridge and Mok (1979) conclude, numerous studies suggest that there are four good reasons for abandoning such assumptions:

1. Few workers are oriented towards maximising their monetary rewards either in the short or long term.
2. Job security is more important than wage differentials.
3. The labour market is opaque rather than transparent and this contributes to the lack of mobility between segments.
4. There is little inclination to move between regions or occupations. (Loveridge and Mok, 1979, pp. 117–18)

In the second place, a number of writers have reported that the actual 'search' for employment, such as it is, is a restricted one particularly for unemployed manual workers (Reynolds, 1951, pp. 85–6; Parker *et al.*, 1971, p. 92; Martin and Fryer, 1973, pp. 138–41). Worker knowledge of what jobs are available, what those jobs entail, what the exact wages might be, or what qualification the employer may be seeking is very limited. Virtually no mechanism exists for the dissemination of this information, beyond a 'Job Centre' system which conveys far less than complete data. This is not surprising, because it is not in the employer's interest to promote one. By restricting knowledge, he is able to constrain the worker's choice, to control access to employment, and to ensure a low turnover of labour. The only avenue open to the rational economic worker would be to sample a number of jobs in order to obtain first-hand experience, but this is likely to be interpreted as an undesirable employment record by the typical prospective employer who is concerned with maintaining a stable work force. Not only is the trial and error approach inconvenient for the worker – despite its 'rationality' – but the superior economic power of the employer enables the latter to block this avenue. However, as Blackburn and Mann observe, the market can operate with workers having a very crude level of knowledge, such as that a firm is offering 'good wages' (Blackburn and Mann, 1979, pp. 15–16).

Just as the worker may have a crude idea about wages and vacancies, he is also likely to have only a partial picture of the way in which

employers differentiate between workers' abilities. While formal
selection criteria exist – education, training, experience, and even
aptitude tests – for many jobs (including some of those in the upper
middle class) the process of selection is haphazard, depending as much
on impressions created during a brief interview with a personnel
manager as anything else. At the manual level, Blackburn and Mann
estimate that in Peterborough 'about 85% of the workers possess the
necessary ability to undertake 95% of jobs' (Blackburn and Mann, 1979,
p. 12). Instead of seeking *quality*, employers 'screen out' workers who
have some attribute which is treated as if it equated with a lack of ability.

> In the first stage of the selection procedure for 'good jobs' are
> weeded out the blacks, the women, those with several jobs over a
> recent short period, the very young and the very old, the single and
> the school dropouts ... What all these criteria have in common is that
> they are aimed less at 'ability' than *stability*. The sought-after
> worker is less the skilful initiative-taking worker than the worker who
> will arrive on time, do as he is told, and not quit. (1979, p. 13)

Selection criteria such as these[2] result in a stratification of the labour
market into at least two sectors. One consists of a market in desirable
jobs sought after by a relatively favoured labour force, while the other
consists of undesirable jobs competed for among sets of stigmatised
labour.

SEGMENTED LABOUR MARKETS

This is the basis for 'segmented' labour market theories, and in
particular dual labour market theory as outlined by Piore (1975).
This postulates a labour market operating as two segments, a primary
sector and a secondary sector. In the first are

> jobs with relatively high wages, good working conditions, chances of
> advancement, equity and due process in the administration of work
> rules and, above all, employment stability. (Piore, 1975, p. 126)

In contrast, jobs in the secondary sector are much more likely to

> be low-paying, with poorer working conditions and little chance of
> advancement: to have a highly personalised relationship between
> workers and supervisors ... and to be characterised by considerable
> instability in jobs and a high turnover among the labour force. (1975,
> p. 126)

Not surprisingly, it is the stigmatised categories of labour which are confined to the secondary sector, and this model has been accordingly directed towards an understanding of poverty and underemployment.

On the demand side, the market is equally segmented. The primary sector is dominated by large monopoly capitalist firms using high technology and which are relatively profitable. They are insulated against short-term fluctuations in demand and so are more concerned with maintaining a stable and experienced workforce which can handle its high technology. The secondary sector consists of firms operating on a smaller scale in a marginal and more chaotic market. Such firms must respond rapidly to changes in market conditions, shedding and re-hiring labour at short notice. As these small firms operate with limited capital, their technology is likely to be low and therefore less dependent on highly specialised labour. Averitt (1965) has expressed this difference as the division under monopoly capitalism into 'core' firms which dominate the primary sector and 'peripheral' firms which operate in the secondary sector, often as subcontractors to the core firms.

It follows that only if certain categories of labour can participate in the primary sector, and if the employers in that sector wish to maintain a stable workforce – with, as we have already noted, only a small proportion of the labour force actively seeking new employment in conditions of low knowledge levels – then the conditions are set for high mutual dependence between employer and worker (Mann, 1973). In such a dual market, a secondary principle comes into operation, the 'internal' labour market. Doeringer and Piore (1971) have suggested that the primary sector consists of a set of internal labour market segments, each consisting of a single firm which controls entry to a range of jobs. Unlike the secondary sector, workers are trained and promoted *within* such a firm, with external recruitment restricted to only certain types of work, most noticeably the most menial. It is possible to regard a particular skill group, already inside a firm, as advantaged by these practices, even if their external movements are restricted. In other words, both employer and employees could benefit from an internal market structure.

This is not the view taken by radical market theorists (see, for example, Edwards *et al.*, 1975). In that formulation, the divisions of the labour market are not merely a contingent result of capitalism, but rather an outcome both necessary for the system's continued existence *and* a deliberate manoeuvre by the capitalist class to weaken the working class. As Blackburn and Mann (1979) have pointed out, this combines functionalist explanation with an excessively conspiratorial theory of history, while at the same time failing to account for the *economic* significance of stigmatised labour. It may be in the *political* interest of the capitalist class to divide the working class against itself, but closer integration of blacks, women, adolescents, etc., into the primary market would force down wage levels and generally weaken the bargaining position of white male workers.

In this discussion of labour markets, the question of ethnic discrimination and migrant labour has largely been omitted for simplification. This should not, however, be taken as implying that the problem is not important: see Moore (1977) and Blackburn and Mann (1979) on which account this section draws. Nor does radical labour market theory explain the variety of practices that can be observed, ranging from active collaboration between workers and employers in maintaining an internal market, to disputes over the restrictive practices of craft unions, and arguments over seniority as a principle of promotion. There has been no single coherent policy on the part of the capitalist class.

The variety of practices is seen as a key element in the critique developed by Loveridge and Mok. While they accept the general points that the labour market discrimination exists in institutionalised form, and that workers seek to maximise their condition, they favour a more complex explanation than that put forward by Doeringer and Piore. Although gender, race, language, age, and religion may all operate as stigmatising characteristics, 'whether the market conditions facing these multi-various groups are sufficiently *homogenous* for them to be considered to be sharing the same market situation is to be doubted' (Loveridge and Mok, 1979, p. 110). Workers experiencing more than one stigma are presumably more disadvantaged than others, while different employers at various times will discriminate on different grounds. A simple dual market model does not adequately encompass this variety.

This critique has been extended by Kaufman *et al.* (1981) who examined segmentation in the US economy using ten broad dimensions ranging over size, capital, control, productivity, unionisation and growth. This enables them to identify eight major segments extending from an 'oligopoly sector' with seven major multinationals, through wholesale and small shop sectors, to utilities and services. Although their prime concern is not employment, their argument that a dual model does not take sufficient account of 'the interaction of profit seeking, technology, environment, union struggle and government intervention', and that such dimensions do not coincide in any simple way, is a powerful one.

What makes their study particularly interesting is that their cluster analysis begins to take on an appearance reminiscent of the industrial sectors discussed in the previous chapter. On the other hand, some of the clusters do strike one as surprising: the similarity of the three sectors 'local monopoly', 'education and non-profit', and 'agricultural' are three strange bed-fellows, sharing low scores on capital intensity, size, concentration and unionisation. Clearly the use of such variables as level of trade union membership or government intervention, which are culturally specific, restricts the precise transfer of conclusion about America to other countries. Nevertheless, Kaufman *et al.*'s analysis reinforces our concern to disaggregate mobility into several industrial sectors as a means of approximating labour markets, and to go beyond a simple dualistic conception.

Mok (1975) has attempted a further variant of the model by suggesting that there are potentially a higher number of labour market segments, with relatively more permeable boundaries. Their exact status depends on the interaction of the primary and secondary markets with the internal labour markets. In two-dimensional terms, one axis expresses how people (or jobs) stand in terms of job rewards, conditions, autonomy and security, while on the other axis people and jobs are characterised by their tasks, skill, training, and place in an organisational hierarchy. The combination of the two dimensions gives the possibility of less attractive labour situations within internal labour markets, and more attractive outside, as well as the more common situation which is the reverse.

One difficulty with these latter views is that the dual labour market model begins to disintegrate into such a segmented structure that all coherence is lost. In that case, any statements are likely to be ones about small clusters of occupations which are linked by the career patterns of individuals. This may not matter in terms of the original labour market debate, in which racial and sexual discrimination loomed very large, but in terms of discovering mobility structures it is something of a disadvantage. If segments of labour market exist, then to be viable for empirical and conceptual use they must be differentiated. That is to say, there must be some degree of segregation between them. The evidence of segregation consists for the most part in differences between wages. For example, Barron and Norris (1976) report an overlap of male and female earnings of less than one-third, but there is less evidence of ethnic segregation in this country, certainly as compared with the USA. Segregation of actual jobs, say by gender, is not always clear cut, if only because conventional categories are too crude to identify the underlying pattern. Nonetheless, there is a concentration of female labour in some occupations, and male labour in others (routine white-collar employment is an obvious example of female concentration: see Clegg and Dunkerley, 1980, pp. 400–5 and Hakim, 1979).

Against this, there is considerable evidence to suggest that segregation is not inherent in the operations of the market *per se*. Differential treatment of the genders is not only rife outside of work, it also predates modern capitalism. Gender segregation of occupations therefore requires no special explanation based on market forces. A parallel argument can be made for ethnic discrimination: arguably there is greater concentration of ethnic groups in education and location of residence than in work.

Again, the segregation of markets implies the allocation of all desirable jobs to the primary sector, and all undesirable jobs to the secondary sector. But there is a hierarchy of desirability *within* both sectors, so that there is penetration of the primary market by stigmatised labour, and of the secondary market by what is assumed to be non-stigmatised labour, i.e. white males. The dual model may hold good at the extremes, but not for the crucial area of the supposed boundary between segments. One reason for this is that the activity of a firm in the primary sector is frequently supported by many small firms which eke out a tenuous existence (in the secondary sector) as subcontractors to the major firm. Some of the occupations, the skills, and the wage rates are common to both, or as one study as part of the Glasgow labour market has shown, the flows of labour between sectors and the complexity of pay structures are so complicated that it is not possible to identify a coherent wage pattern (Robinson, 1970).

The same interconnection also applies between internal and external labour markets. If there were impermeable barriers to an internal market, then labour mobility would be chiefly by means of promotion. Although promotion does take place, it is by no means the dominant process: Mackay *et al.* (1971) report that in the engineering industry 'between firm' moves accounted for more upward mobility than promotion within single operations.

LABOUR MARKETS AND MOBILITY PROCESSES

In the light of this pessimistic appraisal, the reader might be excused for wondering about the value of a lengthy account of labour market theory. The rationale for it consists of two kinds of reasons, those to do with a basic orientation in our approach to the mobility process, and those to do with the more detailed features of the mechanisms by which labour is allocated among occupations.

Once the initial step has been taken towards recognising the centrality of work in understanding mobility, an examination of available models of the work process naturally follows. If labour market theory has failed to provide a complete and tidy explanation, it is not surprising, given the nature of the complex phenomena it attempts to encapsulate. Despite the limitations discussed above, labour market theory is centrally concerned with the forces which determine what jobs people get; it draws attention to the fact that the outcome of the total process depends on the interaction of supply and demand; and (in its segmented form) it delineates the internal subdivisions of the job market. Its utility for mobility analysis is accordingly to reinforce the argument that the economic dimension is of major importance; to demonstrate that access to employment depends both on the availability of, and rules of access to, jobs, as well as the suitability of the would-be workers for those jobs; and to suggest that the mobility competition is not a war of all against all, but rather that the competition tends to be compartmentalised. Not least, labour market theory helps to provide an explanation of *why* mobility takes place, in terms of the central human activity of production, which helps to release mobility research from its relative isolation as a captive of stratification theory.

At a more detailed level, the foregoing discussion suggests several features of *labour markets* which can be explored as *mobility processes*, or more accurately, we can seek empirical evidence as to whether particular mechanisms of job allocation seem to be in operation. The level of analysis and the site restrict what can be done: for example, the occupational segregation of ethnic groups and women cannot be properly analysed with the presently available data. However, if we can legitimately extend the perspective to the rest of the labour force, and in particular to unskilled manual workers, then the connection can be made. Piore (1975) has suggested in passing that both class and mobility can be related to main segments of the labour market. Although it is not his main concern, he distinguishes three segments – an upper and lower primary sector, and a secondary sector – which comprise types of work corresponding to middle classes, working class, and lower class subcultures, the latter being sociological categories (1975, p. 128). In the course of careers, if not at entry, people from middle-class backgrounds gravitate to upper primary types of work, while those from working-class origins come to occupy the lower primary jobs and the lower classes end up in the secondary market. In the more familiar mobility terminology, Piore is suggesting that the effect of family background is not greatest at first job (as is normally assumed in mobility analysis informed by ideas of ascription giving way to achievement) but rather at the 'present job'. The mechanics of this are not spelt out, but appear to reside in the fact that the middle class in particular enter occupations which are part of a cluster of jobs comprising a mobility chain, that is, they have careers. Such mobility chains are concentrated in the upper primary sector. The validity of this model can be tested by comparing mobility at different points in the career.

A second concrete proposition which can be tested is drawn from Loveridge and Mok (1979). Developing Mok's earlier two-dimensional, four-segment model, they argue that the segment with higher wages, better working conditions, higher unionisation, involving sophisticated technology, autonomy, and high levels of internal promotion are concentrated in the following industries: oil, chemicals, public utilities, and metallurgy. Conversely, the segment with lower wages, poorer working conditions etc are to be found in textiles, leather goods, glassware and food (interestingly, not in service occupations). In principle, a mobility analysis should also be able to examine similar industrial groupings and also to use this proposition as a special case of Piore's argument above.

Third, and more generally, if the internal/external market concept is taken seriously it means that promotion should feature predominantly in the explanations respondents give for their job changes. This shifts attention away from pre-work attributes like education, and towards intra-career events. Similarly, the logic of a secondary and external sector can be extended to those who have no skills but only muscle power to sell. We would expect to find these categories of worker concentrated in certain industries, such as manufacturing rather than service industry. Similarly, number of jobs held – as respondent attributes – should be correlated with type of industry and class position. If there is a segmented labour market, mobility can be used as a measure of that segmentation, in the same way that mobility is used to identify class boundaries. Thus if there is evidence of segmentation, we can examine careers to find whether those presently occupying segments have ever worked in other sectors of the market. To quote Jain and Sloane (1977, p. 4), 'the essence of segmentalist theories is the all pervasive nature of barriers to mobility' (mobility here having a wider meaning than social mobility). This in turn links back to our discussion of Parkin and Giddens' views of class and strategies of closures, although we now have a more elaborated version of the processes at work to create stratification. By taking account of these various factors, the way is open for both mobility analysis, and of providing some evidence on labour markets (see Payne, 1986, for details). The theory of industry society offers is a number of perspectives by which stratification can be linked, through mobility and occupations, to the historically unique feature of advanced technology. In Chapters 4 and 5 we have been less concerned with class *per se* than occupation, but the nature of the upper middle class emerges from the early section as being particularly problematic – as indeed it did from the discussion in Chapter 3. At the same time, the present account has argued for an analysis which goes beyond broad statements about technology and society, or industrial sectors, to examine in greater detail how different sectors, with their characteristic technologies, create occupational demands. This approach assumes a somewhat less integrated and untidy character for industrial society than some earlier writers, with various sectors being 'more advanced' than others. Regional variations in industrial mix are seen as an important example of this, but in the more general case, the overall patterns of employment and mobility may respond to changes which operate only in one (or a few) of the several sectors. To put it another way, trends and counter-trends are not society-wide phenomena, but can be located in areas and industries. It follows that the class structure of a society is seen primarily as an aggregation of these many labour/technology (and organisational) processes, rather than having an objective existence in its own right.

It should now be clear that we have come a long way from conventional views of social mobility as primarily a class process. While mobility must still be about social class, it can now be seen as a more complex phenomenon that cannot be totally contained within a class framework, which is precisely how it has been constrained by British writing on mobility. However, the problem of such writing is not just that it has been conceptually limited. In addition, almost all of this body of work has directly or indirectly used the 1954 LSE mobility study as evidence on which to base its conclusions. Not only was this evidence collected long ago (in 1949) but as we shall see in the next chapter, there are sufficient doubts about its accuracy to indicate the need for a complete theoretical *and* empirical reappraisal of class and mobility.

6 *Social Mobility in Britain*: The Old Evidence

There can be few areas of British sociology that are so dominated by one study, as social mobility is dominated by David Glass's *Social Mobility in Britain* (1954).[1] In the twenty years that followed the appearance of this book, there were only a handful of mobility publications which did not rely on Glass for their empirical evidence, and those few that disagreed with the LSE study – such as Benjamin (1958) and Noble (1972 and 1975a) – were largely ignored. Leading English writers in the field of social class such as Bottomore (1965), Westergaard and Resler (1975), Worsley *et al.* (1977), Parkin (1971), and Giddens (1973) all quote Glass (or more precisely, Miller's (1960) reworking of the Glass data, as the foundation of their ideas about rates of mobility. As one key figure in the second generation of mobility studies, Keith Hope, observed in 1974, Glass has

> contributed materially to the theoretical debate on British stratification. Indeed, theories of British occupational mobility, so far from being derived from some broad body of speculative sociology, have tended to ground themselves in an agreed reading of the findings of the 1949 inquiry, differing from one another only in the supposed mechanisms and processes which they postulate to explain those findings. (Hope, 1975, pp. 1–2)

It would not be an exaggeration to say that for over twenty years Glass was to social mobility what Darwin was to the theory of evolution.

How are we to explain this? First, there is the kind of usage to which Glass's data were put. British sociology has been centrally concerned with social class, and social mobility was subsumed under that heading. There was almost no interest in occupational mobility *per se*: evidence about recruitment patterns relied for its significance on what it could tell sociology about class boundaries and the continuity of the class structure. Because mobility assumed only a secondary importance to sociologists more concerned with social class (such as the writers mentioned above) they were content to take Glass's evidence on trust. The prime focus of their work, social class, provided ample problems, so that there was little incentive to become deeply involved in the detailed technicalities of social mobility, which, after all, comprised only one element of the total picture.

In the second place, Glass's study was highly plausible, both in its methodology and its findings. On the one hand, the study was an exceptionally sophisticated one, even by today's standards. It had a large sample with national coverage (3497 male respondents in England and Wales, and 417 in Scotland (Glass, 1954, pp. 180–3 and pp. 213–15). Its statistical innovations not only took up several chapters but formed the basis of much later developments on mobility indices in Britain and abroad. Hauser (1978), for example, has commented that even if doubts have been expressed about *Social Mobility in Britain*, the source is so well known that it is best to continue using it for statistical development. On technical grounds, it was an unimpeachable source, particularly during a period of sociology's history in this country, when statistical expertise was not an essential part of the sociologist's repertoire. Albeit in a slightly different context, Keith Hope (1975) has suggested that it was Glass's development of statistics based on a X^2 model that had great influence: even non-numerate sociologists could follow a X^2 approach in a general sense. David Glass's numerical expertise as a demographer also probably helped to promote confidence in his mobility results.

On the other hand, its findings made sense. Almost without exception, sociological writers on social class in Britain have adopted a political stance on the Left. When Glass wrote that there was little upward social mobility, it reinforced everything else that they knew about the class system. There was no incentive, therefore, to challenge his results. What is more, Glass's 'hard' scientific evidence was a great support both in the debate with Conservative Party ideologues, and with liberal apologists for capitalism. Even US sociology welcomed Glass's findings as helping to show the difference between an open and achievement-dominated society like that of the USA, and closed class-ridden societies in Europe (e.g. Bendix and Lipset, 1959).

There is, however, a third and more important reason why *Social Mobility in Britain* has been so influential, and that is the position of the sponsoring institution, LSE. To understand this it is necessary to look at the state of English early post-war sociology. The frequent comment that sociology is a relatively new discipline is more true than is normally recognised: in Britain the profession has existed for all intents and purposes for a bare thirty or forty years. The growth of sociology is quite remarkable. In the last full year before the outbreak of the Second

World War there were only 35 professors in *all* of the social sciences in Britain, and 177 lecturing staff on other grades (Clapham, 1946). The number of graduating students in sociology, anthropology and social administration combined was just 33 (Heyworth, 1965). By 1973, there were around 12,000 sociology teachers in higher education, and another 900 sociologists in research work. Indeed a 1975 survey of only nineteen polytechnics found more sociologists than all social scientists in 1938/9 (Nicholas, 1978). By 1970, there were 1700 graduates a year in sociology and social anthropology, while five years later there were over 2500 social science postgraduates (Smith, 1973: HMSO, 1975).

Before this rapid growth, British sociology was synonymous with LSE, where the dominant mode until the late 1940s was more of social philosophy and ethics. The central figures among the 'old guard' at LSE were Marshall, Ginsberg and Mannheim. These men represented continuity with the early years of British sociology, both in their experience and also in terms of what they were teaching. Mannheim taught a theory course while Ginsberg was centrally concerned with Hobhouse's style of sociology.

A student of that period has remarked that, in teaching theory and method together, Ginsberg was strong on methodology at the level of philosophy of science, but less so on techniques of data-collection. In most respects this was the final flowering of the old sociology, for there was an abrupt change in the early 1950s, shortly after the arrival of David Glass. Largely under the influence of Shils, US sociology was introduced to the School. Both Parsonian functionalism and a watered-down version of Lazarsfeldian empiricism were suddenly challengers to social Darwinism and civic sociology (Halsey, 1982). These new doctrines were taken up by a particularly good crop of graduates and young staff in the early post-war years: for example, Asher Tropp, Cyril Smith, Chelly Halsey, Joe and Olive Banks. Many of these were the 'young turks' who were to determine the future direction of the new British Sociological Association towards a professional association (Banks, 1967). These sociologists made successful careers and were influential in setting up new departments in other universities. For a number of years, LSE could boast that half of the sociology chairs in Britain were filled by LSE graduates.

During the explosion of sociology in the late 1960s, successive generations of LSE students, postgraduates, research assistants and junior lecturers became the staff of other newly developed departments. Not least among these were Glass's co-researchers who went on to become heads of department: Kelsall, Martin, Floud, Halsey, Banks and Banks, and Bottomore. They took with them an interpretation of social mobility which was unusually coherent, and until the 1970s there was a general assumption that mobility 'had been done' by Glass, and that there was little more to be said on the subject.

These conventional interpretations of mobility contain several interrelated strands. First, mobility is normally taken to mean exchange mobility rather than structural mobility: that is, mobility refers to those movements between occupation statuses over and above any movements 'necessitated' by a change in the occupational structure between the father's and the son's generations. Second, while recognising that movements do frequently occur, it has been generally agreed that movements over the whole range of the occupational structure are very rare. The typical move is a 'short distance' one; the clerk's son who becomes a departmental manager, or the miner's son who becomes a clerk. Third, social mobility has been subsumed under a wider concern with the contemporary class structure: in so far as it has been of interest to British sociologists, it has been only as a contributory factor in the structured inequality of life chances, and in class formation. It has not been of much interest in its own right, or in a comparative context. In short, a dominant paradigm has existed for over twenty years in British sociology which drew heavily on Glass, but which, in its acceptance of Glass's findings, generated little significant new research or speculation about mobility patterns *per se* until the present round of studies.

If there is any doubt about this, consider the way in which three recent and well-regarded writers on the sociology of stratification have dismissed mobility as a constant and known process. Westergaard and Resler (1977) discuss Glass's results, concluding that there has been

> no change of substance in the amount of movement up and down the social scale till about the time of World War II. And there seems now to have been little increase in social circulation after that either . . . Long distance movement especially – from bottom to top, as well as from top to bottom – is uncommon. Most individual mobility is far more modest; and much of it stays on one side or the other of the conventional dividing line between white- and blue-collar work. (Westergaard and Resler, 1977, pp. 315 and 302)

Second, Scase, in a review of *Class in a Capitalist Society* in *Sociolgy* approves of Westergaard and Resler's section on mobility as scotching the popular myth of a more open society, and thereby confirming 'what every sociologist knows' [Sic] (Scase, 1976, p. 515). Certainly, this is the view presented to many beginning students of sociology: the second edition of Worsley's *Introducing Sociology*, which claims that its first edition 'has been used in about half the universities in the UK, in many colleges of various kinds, and even – to our surprise – in schools' (Worsley *et al.* 1977; p. 15), asserts that

> though there is a great deal of mobility, most of it is, in fact, very short range mobility. The myths of 'long distance' mobility – 'from log-cabin to President' – are, overwhelmingly, myths as far as the life chances of the mass of the population are concerned. (Worsley *et al.* 1977, p. 432)

The authors continue by quoting verbatim Westergaard and Resler's version of stable mobility rates referred to above.

These three sources, with their dependence on Glass, lend support to the view that there has been an agreed and widely held notion of mobility among British sociologists. Indeed, the same statements about limited and short range mobility can be found with only very slight variation in the works of Bottomore (1965; p. 38); Miliband (1969, pp. 34–44); Parkin (1971, pp. 51–6); Miller (1960, pp. 36–41); Raynor (1969, pp. 33–5); Frankel (1969, p. 161); Goldthorpe (1974, pp. 145–6) and Giddens (1973, p. 107 and pp. 181–2). We shall return to the detail of what these writers say about mobility on page 129.

It will become apparent from the foregoing pages that *Social Mobility in Britain* is of such importance that it must be the starting point for any subsequent study of social mobility. If one is to propose findings that challenge those of Glass, one must be on the strongest of grounds, and given the security of his reputation, one is placed in the position of needing to marshal every possible argument to counter his case, and indeed the case of all those other subsequent sociologists who have based their ideas upon his evidence. It is a daunting task.

There are at least four different critiques of Glass that could be adopted. The first, and simplest, is that if more recent studies disagree with Glass, then the explanation lies in changes in British society since 1949 when the fieldwork for the first study was done. If rates of mobility are found to be higher in the 1970s, than around 1950, both findings can be assumed to be accurate for their respective times. This is the view espoused by Goldthorpe and Llewellyn (1977) who argue that Glass's study came by mischance just at the end of an era of low mobility, whereas their Nuffield study in 1972 taps the subsequent era of higher mobility.

An alternative view is the one which will take up much of the final section of this chapter. That is, that the Glass findings are in some way inaccurate. In this case, the more recent studies (of England and Wales, and of Scotland) represent the first accurate studies of their kind.

In fact, the present author adopts a third position, namely one that draws on the previous two. If changes in mobility rates depend on real historical events like the availability of employment or the growth of white-collar occupations, then inevitably Glass's findings would be specific to the time at which the LSE research was carried out. Equally, if there are reasons to doubt its accuracy, its results may be biased in some way. The two conditions are in no way mutually exclusive.

There is an additional independent critique which applies only to Scotland. Even if the case for questioning Glass's account of *English* mobility is not proven – which of course is not the position taken in this chapter – then the problems with Glass's treatment of his Scottish data remain. As this is an argument of lesser importance than the more fundamental question of accuracy, it will not be dealt with here (see Payne *et al.*, 1976).

GLASS ON ENGLAND AND WALES: OCCUPATIONAL TRANSITION

It is often the case with seminal works that any technical defects or limitations are quickly overlooked and soon conveniently forgotten. Glass himself took great pains to point out a number of unusual features of his results, and later writers (mainly in the field of social mobility, rather than class theory *per se*) have echoed his observations. However, very little has been done to consider what significance such features might have. For example, it is almost a commonplace that the LSE mobility tables are unusually symetrical, or that class differentials in fertility rates produce a biased distribution of fathers' occupations – both points originally made by Glass. Other peculiarities have been reported by Ridge and Hope during the recent phase of national mobility studies. But as yet, these problems have not collectively received the attention which they merit; the intention of this chapter is to remedy this, and thereby to raise doubts about the uses to which the Glass data have been put by later writers, i.e. in conceptualising the British class structure.

The starting point of this reappraisal is the core of mobility analysis, the mobility table. One of the general characteristics of mobility tables showing respondents' occupations tabulated by their fathers' occupations is that the distribution of occupations for the respondents is different from that of their fathers. The dominant pattern of such tables is that fewer of the fathers have middle-class occupations than do the respondents (or sons), and conversely more fathers appear to be in working-class occupations. This pattern is associated with greater overall upward occupational mobility than downward mobility despite varying levels of inherited advantage and self-recruitment, and is commonly found in national mobility tables for twentieth-century industrial societies.

There are two major reasons why the fathers/sons distributions differ in this respect; changes in occupational structure and differences in fertility. The thesis of occupation transition, discussed above, that industrial societies manifest a trend towards increasing skill levels, with more professional, technical and white-collar workers, and relatively fewer unskilled manual workers, implies a steady expansion of the more desirable middle-class occupations. This necessitates a flow of workers into those new occupations which expand the middle-class sector. In other words, the sons of working-class families are less likely to inherit their fathers' jobs because relatively speaking, the working-class sector is contracting while the middle-class sector is expanding, thereby making it easier to enter. This process is reinforced by educational policies designed to produce a workforce with the necessary skills for further vocational specialisation. The result is structural mobility, which mobility researchers since the mid-1970s have increasingly seen as the major component of mobility (e.g. Hauser *et al.*, 1975a and 1975b; Goldthorpe, 1980a; Hope, 1980).

In mainland Britain, for example, professional, technical, supervisory and routine white-collar male workers increased from about 3.9 million in 1921 to over 6.9 million in 1971, and have become 45 per cent of all jobs compared with 30 per cent, as Table 6.1 shows.

Blue-collar workers, despite an absolute increase in numbers between 1921 and 1951, have been in relative decline since the First World War, and absolute decline since 1951. Their proportion of the classified workforce has fallen from 70 per cent to under 55 per cent (excluding armed forces). The process of occupational transition can be traced back into the nineteenth century, although the mechanics of this exercise are not easy. The technical aspects of using census data to construct a time series become more difficult, because job titles (and work tasks) become more different the further back one goes. It seems that the rate of change increases in this century, but there is no evidence of a reversal of the occupational transition process in the later part of the previous century.

Table 6.1 Occupational transition in Scotland, England and Wales in 1921, 1951 and 1971: economically active males, aged 20–64*

		1921	%	1951	%	1971	%
'White Collar' Occupations SEG 1–6; 8; 12–14 (incl. Farmers)	Scotland	419,641	28.3	480,729	31.2	560,890	39.1
	England & Wales	3,519,704	30.0	4,706,004	35.1	6,386,250	45.8
	Total	3,939,345	29.8	5,186,733	34.7	6,947,140	45.2
'Blue Collar' Occupations SEG 7; 9–11; 15	Scotland	1,063,192	71.7	1,060,221	68.8	872,040	60.9
	England & Wales	8,225,290	70.0	8,713,168	64.9	7,566,240	54.2
	Total	9,288,482	70.2	9,773,389	65.3	8,438,280	54.8
Totals (excluding armed forces & SEG 17 (not known))	Scotland	1,482,833	100	1,540,950	100	1,432,930	100
	England & Wales	11,744,994	100	13,419,172	100	13,952,490	100
	Total	13,227,827	100	14,960,122	100	15,385,420	100

*Throughout this section, data are presented in broad categories such as 'White-collar' or 'Manual' workers in order to achieve comparability over the several studies.

SOURCE: adapted from Census Occupational Tables.

In samples of fathers and sons, we would therefore expect to find differences in occupational status. Men starting careers in 1920 say, joined a labour market which had greater demand for manual labour than did the labour market of 1950. In other words, the father was more likely to start as a manual labourer in 1920 (and therefore to remain one or at least to have a harder task of subsequently getting a non-manual career) while his son had a better chance of entering white-collar work in 1950. This is reflected in mobility tables, but will be distorted by other factors (particularly differential fertility as we shall shortly see below). Table 6.2 gives three examples from more recent surveys.

These three recent examples provide some indication that sons have a better chance of obtaining white-collar jobs, but we need to look at this in more detail than just at the level of probabilities. Underpinning the effect are the actual social processes through which individuals enter occupations. The allocation mechanism ensures that only individuals with certain attributes may enter given occupations: race, gender, and educational qualifications are obvious examples of entry attributes.

Table 6.2   Occupational distributions of generations (%)*

	Generation	Non-Manual	Manual
Scotland 1975	fathers	34.5	65.5
n=4468	sons	46.2	53.8
England & Wales 1972	fathers	46.1	53.9
n=9423	sons	55.3	44.7
USA 1962	fathers	29.5	70.5
n=27,592	sons	39.6	60.4

*Different classification schemes make the comparisons approximate only.

SOURCES: Scotland: Scottish Mobility Study data.
England: Goldthorpe and Llewellyn (1977, p. 273) (non-manual=I–V inc.).
USA: Blau and Duncan (1967, p. 496) (excludes 'farmers'; non-manual=1–7 inclusive).

Although people do change their occupations, these changes are not random: not only are some occupations barred because the basic entry attributes are different, but the individual's own work experience rapidly becomes a further occupational entry attribute. For example, the skilled manual worker in a factory may subsequently become a foreman and even a manager in that company or industry, but he does not suddenly become a brain surgeon. To do that he would have to retrain and start again at the bottom. His skills are not transferable. Nor can the highly educated brain surgeon easily obtain a job on a building site should he wish it, even though the builder's labourer has few formal skills and the trade has a tradition of high labour turnover. Faced with two job applicants, a choice between an experienced builder's labourer and the unknown quantity, an ex-brain surgeon, the typical employer will opt for the devil he knows.

In other words, occupations are organised into 'channels', with very limited interconnection between each channel, or to use Stewart *et al.*'s (1980) simile taking up an occupation is like starting on a train journey: once started, it is hard to reach any other destination, despite a number of junctions in the rail system. Because men become caught up in the occupational system, it is not easy for the labour force as a whole to adapt quickly to new demands for a different kind of skill. Popular political and journalistic comment about the current need to retrain and change occupations in mid-career fails to recognise the human investment that goes into twenty years of working in one job, or rather in one occupational channel. The very limited success of government retraining programmes in the last two decades is another indication of the rigidity of these channels, even for workers whose skills and experience are now surplus to requirements. Both trade unions and employers play key roles in maintaining the boundaries of these channels. Rather than mature workers transferring from one old channel to a new one, it is easier to divert some of the newcomers to the labour market. This protects the incumbents of a declining channel, and reduces the intensity of the inevitable dislocation of redundancy. It is also easier to set up, as the educational system is geared to younger people and can be adapted to provide new training and careers counselling. Apart from a brief interim period before a new occupation is identified, employers in expanding job sectors turn to the new generation for its recruits. To take one example close to home, the occupation of sociologist rapidly passed through an era in which its recruits were converted from other disciplines such as history, philosophy, and even engineering, into the golden sixties when the *majority* of present members entered the profession directly through the newly created departments of sociology in the post-Robbins Universities and Polytechnics (Payne *et al.*, 1981).

In sum, the differences between fathers and sons do not lie only in a simple stochastic process, but also in the workings of the relevant institutions. As the occupational structure changes, its effects impinge most immediately on young workers, for whom new opportunities open up more readily than for older workers. As a result, there is a built-in potential for upward social mobility, as blue-collar trades contract, and new white-collar trades expand.

DIFFERENTIAL FERTILITY

However, the figures that we saw in Table 6.2 do not derive solely from this underlying process of occupational transition. A second historically specific process which gives rise to differences between the fathers' and sons' distributions as seen in mobility tables is differential fertility. Broadly speaking, working-class fathers each have more children (and therefore, of course, more sons) than do middle-class fathers. A sample of the sons would find more who said their fathers were working class, because there would be a greater chance of working-class sons being sampled. This would lead to an overestimate of the proportion of working-class fathers (Glass, 1954, p. 191).

Consider the following example: suppose there were only two classes, A and B, of equal size, and the population remained unchanged over two generations; but class A fathers had on average one child each (0.5 sons per father), while class B fathers each had on average three children (1.5 sons per father). We draw a sample of eight sons and ask them about their fathers. Regardless of the occupations of the sons, the distribution for eight fathers would be:

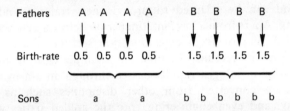

6 out of 8 sons (the b's) would say that their fathers were class B, and only 2 out of 8 (the a's) would declare class A. Therefore our estimate of the fathers' occupational distribution on the basis of the sons' answers would not be 50:50 but 25:75 (for further discussion see Allan and Bytheway, 1973).

In other words, we would expect a mobility table to exaggerate the proportion of fathers with manual jobs (because they have larger families), so that even with *no* real occupational transition, there would be an appearance of difference between the fathers' and sons' occupational distributions, such that more of the sons seemed to be in non-manual employment.

As a concrete illustration, the fertility for women married between 1900 and 1909 was 2.64 for R–G Class I, ranging to 4.17 for R–G Class V. Marriages contracted between 1927 and 1931 (and enumerated 20–24 years later) produced from 1.88 to 3.18 children for the same classes (Carr-Saunders *et al.*, 1958, p. 25). To some extent these differences in crude averages are 'damped down' by infant mortality, so that 1.88 becomes 1.78 while 3.18 becomes 2.74 (Ministry of Health, 1956, p. 233) and the rate for sons becomes thereby approximately 0.89 (below full self-replacement) and 1.37. The manual/non-manual 'differential' has been 'remarkably constant in relative terms, over the early part of this century' at around 1.9 and 2.7 live born children (Carr-Saunders *et al.*, 1958, p. 24).

Unfortunately, it is not possible to relate these changes in a direct way to the Glass mobility table for England and Wales. In practice, Glass's 'generation' of sons was aged from 20 to 64 in 1949, that is, born between 1885 and 1929. Thus the fertility rates cover a span of 44 years, during which time they were changing. As Glass himself has indicated elsewhere, the fertility differential between manual and non-manual classes was about 1.2:1 for marriages in the 1870s and increased to about 1.4:1 around the time of the Great Depression (Glass, 1969, p. 44 and private correspondence, 1976). The published information on this is somewhat limited, and moreover, is presented in terms of several classifications, including the Registrar-General's class schema. It is remarkable how little this topic appears in otherwise lengthy discussions of fertility (see, for example, Hawthorn, 1970; Busfield and Paddon, 1977; Cotgrove, 1967, and other commentators on Bank's 1954 thesis on class differentials in fertility). It is therefore not possible to specify the effect of differential fertility on the mobility table without a very considerable and intensive study, including the reclassification of original records, which lies outside of the focus of the present work, combined with a year-by-year matching of each annual component of the sample with its relevant class fertility rate. The situation on the occupational transition dimensions is even poorer: there is no year-to-year data, so that one is dependent on census data available only at ten-year intervals. Inevitably we must be contented with an approximation.

Glass's sons were born from the 1880s on, i.e. in the period when the class differential in fertility was in excess of 1.35:1.0 (Glass and Grebennick, 1954). Furthermore, the bulk of the increase in the differential was achieved by the early years of this century (Carr-Saunders *et al.*, 1958, quoted above). About two-thirds of Glass's sample was born after 1900, so that we can set the approximate average differential for the whole period as $(1 \times 1.35)+(2 \times 1.42)/3=1.397$. This slightly underestimates the differential: therefore if we take the figure of 1.4:1 as applying throughout the period, we have an estimate which is still a cautious one, even allowing something for class differential in mortality, (obviously the average differential between the extremes, say R–G's Class I and Class V, could be calculated in basically the same fashion and would be much greater).

Thus we can argue that if we treat the *reported* number of non-manual fathers as a base figure for the real number in the father's generation, then the number of reported manual fathers overestimates the real number by a factor of 1.4. In other words, the 2199 'manual' fathers (i.e. using Miller's (1960) version of Glass's data, as against Glass's categories 5, 6 and 7 which actually include routine white-collar occupations) reported in the sample represents 1571 in the real distribution. This would give an occupational structure in which there were really 54.8 per cent manual and 45.2 per cent non-manual fathers, instead of the 62.9 per cent and 37.1 per cent in the reported case. The estimate of 8.1 per cent difference in the proportions could, of course, have been derived from taking the reported number of *manual* fathers as the base and *weighting up* the non-manual reported figure instead.[2]

While it is useful to obtain this estimate, the more significant point of this argument is the general one that the reported difference between fathers' and sons' occupational distributions underestimates the number of middle-class fathers and overestimates the number of working-class fathers. It therefore creates a picture in which there appears to be even more intergenerational occupational transition than is in fact the case, which in turn generates more upward mobility. The occupational transition effect and the class differentials in fertility are complementary.

FATHERS' AND SONS' DISTRIBUTION IN GLASS'S DATA

The effects of these processes should be evident in the following distributions of fathers and sons taken from the LSE study: the dotted line indicates the middle-class boundary. Table 6.3 is not a mobility table; it says nothing about how pairs of fathers and sons fit into particular classes, because the two columns are discrete.

It will be immediately apparent that the two distributions do *not* differ greatly from one another, and that the difference between them in 5 out of 7 classes is not as expected. Classes 1, 3 and 4 of the middle-class sector show *more* fathers than sons, while working classes 6 and 7 show *fewer* fathers than sons. If we split Class 5 into white-collar and skilled manual (following Miller, 1960, p. 71), then routine white collar shows more sons than fathers, 244 to 156, and skilled manual shows fewer sons, 1185 to 1354, both differences being in the expected direction. However, on the basis of Miller's conversion, fathers and sons are almost exactly equal: a difference of only three cases between number of non-manual fathers and non-manual sons.

But it is known that all these figures distort the real distribution because of differential fertility, so that actual situation is one in which there are generally even more middle-class occupations in the father's generation than shown, and even fewer working-class occupations. So

Table 6.3. Occupational distributions of fathers and sons in *Social Mobility in Britain*

	Father's occupation as reported by son	Son's occupation as reported by son
1. Professionals	129	103
2. Managerial/executive	150	159
3. Higher non-manual/supervisory	345	330
4. Lower non-manual/supervisory	518	459
5. Routine non-manual/skilled manual	1510	1429
6. Semi-skilled manual	458	593
7. Unskilled manual	387	424
Totals	3497	3497

SOURCE: Glass, 1954, pp. 180–8.

the full extent of the difference is underestimated. The Glass mobility table appears to refer to a society at a time when the middle class has contracted and the working class expanded, against the thesis of occupational transition.

However, as we earlier showed from census data, for at least the last thirty years of the period covered by Glass (i.e. the period including for most of the sample the reported 'father's job'), there was an expansion of the middle class. Thus it can be concluded that on the one hand there is census evidence of *an expansion of perhaps as much as 17 per cent*, controlling for population growth, while on the other hand the Glass data show a *contraction of 18 per cent*.[3] Even if the exact magnitudes of these percentages are based on approximation, it still seems reasonable to raise questions about the validity of the sample data.

To what extent can Glass's data be reconciled with these doubts? In the first place, we need to eliminate one tempting possibility: artefactual distortion due to definitions. Unlike his successors, Glass operationalises mobility by comparing the sons' occupations with the last known occupations of the fathers (Glass, 1954, p. 179). Later studies have used an earlier occupational status for the fathers, namely a job point during the sons' later schooldays, such as when the sons were aged 14 (or less commonly, 16). This has the advantage of connecting father and son sociologically, as the impact of family background is at its greatest when both father and son are members of one household, and the son is at a crucial stage of his education. It also allows for the use of path analysis, since the logically prior father's occupation can be shown to be chronologically prior. It has the disadvantage, compared with Glass, that the father may yet experience more mobility between the time when his son is 14 and the end of his own career, so distorting the measurement of mobility. In fact, the average age of the father when his son was 14 would be in the late forties, so that a degree of stabilisation would have already occurred. The weight of advantage seems to lie in the operationalisation of father's job at the time his son was about 14, which has almost universally been adopted.

In the present context, it might be argued that by Glass's taking the fathers later in life, they would be more advanced in their careers and so more represented among the non-manual sector. This might account for the symmetry of the mobility table. There is no precise answer to this suggestion, although there is indirect evidence to the contrary. First, we have just observed, the fathers' careers are on average well advanced by the time their sons reach 14 years old: Glass suggests 34 for the age of the father at the birth of his mid-child, which means 48 years old by the time the mid-child is 14 (1954, p. 191). As we shall see for Scotland in the section on *intra*generational mobility, most careers have run their course by this stage. On the basis of Harris and Clausen's *Labour Mobility in Great Britain* (1966) Goldthorpe (1980a) has recently argued that by the time men are aged 35 and over, they

> will tend to have achieved a stage of relative 'occupational maturity', in the sense that from then onwards one may expect if not a cessation at all events a marked falling off in the probability of job changes which involve major shifts in occupational level. (1980a, pp. 51–2)

We would therefore expect little difference to emerge from the use of different time points.

A second indirect source is the 1975 mobility data for Scotland. As Table 6.4 shows, the predicted pattern of differences in the two distributions is present when 'father's *last* job' is compared with that of the son. There is one exception: class 6, semi-skilled manual, where instead of there being fewer sons than fathers, there are 25 more. However, each of the other classes does fit, and the overall non-manual percentages are 35.3 per cent for the fathers and 46.3 per cent for the sons. If one had used the father's job when the son was 14, the comparable percentages would be 34.5 per cent and 46.3 per cent and all seven of the classes follow the expected pattern. Despite the common-sense expectation that the greater difference between the distribution,

Table 6.4 Occupational distributions of fathers and sons in Scottish Mobility Study, 1975

Occupational Class*	Father's last occupation as reported by son	Son's current occupation as reported by son
1. Professional/managerial	303	550
2. Semi-professionals, supervisory	585	689
3. Foremen, s.e: artisans	585	645
4. Routine white collar	168	267
Non-manual subtotals	1641 (35.3%)	2151 (46.3%)
5. Skilled manual	1088	940
6. Semi-skilled manual	872	897
7. Unskilled manual	1047	660
Manual subtotals	3007 (64.7%)	2497 (53.7%)
Totals	4648	4648

*Classes not those used by Glass.

the greater the mobility, such as the detailed changes that there is marginally *more* mobility when one uses the father's last job as the destination. On these several items of indirect evidence it is concluded that choice of job point for the father does not account for Glass's data being a 'deviant' case-

GLASS'S EXPLANATION OF HIS RESULTS

It should be recognised that Glass himself was aware of the problems with his data and attempted to deal with them, although with only partial success. Indeed, his explanations may have unwittingly contributed to later misinterpretations of his position, because he stressed the stability of the occupational structure and suggested that differential fertility was a phenomenon the impact of which is minimised by its occurring mainly in the recent past:

Mortality is correlated negatively with social status, but so is fertility, so that the two factors will tend to counteract one another. It is unlikely, however, that they will completely cancel each other.

> Having regard for the historical development of social status differences in fertility, it is more probable that, relatively, the bias towards the representation of 'manual' fathers will be greater on the more recent than the earlier cohorts. (Glass, 1954, p. 191)

In view of the little attention that it received from later commentators, Glass's discussion of this appears to have been taken as implying that the class fertility differential is not too important, because of the late appearance of the differential, and the countervailing affect of mortality. However, as we have shown above, the fertility differentials do affect the whole sample, and adjustment for mortality only very partially counteracts the differential (see Glass, 1969, p. 44, and Parker *et al.*, 1972). It follows that the differences in fertility effect between the early and late cohorts covers more of the sample than some later commentators may have taken Glass to mean.

Glass also recognises the occupational basis of the discrepant father/son pattern, but while accepting that it appears unusual, he goes on to argue that it represents a genuine change in the social structure of Britain. He writes that the data suggest

> a slight decline in the opportunities for high status over time, a decline which appears in the data for the subjects' fathers as well as for the subjects themselves . . . the most likely conclusion is that there was no important change between 1911 and 1941 in the proportion of 'non-manual' employment for the [fathers] concerned . . . the increase in the proportions of 'manual' occupations – and therefore of occupations of relatively low rank in the prestige hierarchy – as the more recent decades of birth are approached, is genuine. (Glass, 1954, p. 190 and pp. 192–4)

Thus Glass accepts his data as being valid, even if 'somewhat unexpected' and requiring some justification. He argues that his finding of a contraction of middle-class opportunity is not necessarily

> in conflict with the known fact that certain specific types of white collar occupations have greatly expanded over the past fifty years. It would mean, however, that other occupations of comparable status have contracted to an even greater extent. And also that the expanded opportunities in certain white collar occupations have been taken over by women. (Glass, 1954, p. 190)

But he does not elaborate on which specific occupations he has in mind, and he does not relate his findings to the thesis of occupational transition, although of course the state of such theories in the 1950s was less advanced than the present day. Instead, he uses the 1951 Census data as a comparison, or as Ridge has noted in the context of discussing peculiarities of brother/subject/father differences, the original investigators

> seem to have been somewhat surprised, and attempted by manipulations of census statistics to show that the same trend can be observed on a status scale other than that of Hall and Jones. (Ridge, 1974b, p. 91)

Glass and his colleagues present two tables of comparison with the 1951 Census, one for the fathers and one for the subjects. Since the argument is essentially the same for both, we shall deal mainly with the latter, because the data on the fathers are a poor estimate of true occupational distribution due to the differential fertility factor.

Glass claims that the occupational structure has led to an increase in categories 4 to 7 inclusive ('manual') in his sample, from 78.7 per cent for the oldest ten-year cohort, to 89 per cent for the youngest cohort, with a consistent trend for each cohort in between. The form 'manual' is adopted to emphasise that, strictly speaking, Glass is not talking about manual workers but a somewhat larger category including some lower white-collar workers. He compares this with 1951 data (i.e. from a single census) showing that the R-G's social classes 3 to 5 inclusive (again 'manual') has similar scores of 78.4 per cent to 87.7 per cent for the same cohorts. This is shown in Table 6.5.

Table 6.5   Proportions of 'manual' respondents in four cohorts as reported in *Social Mobility in Britain*

	Glass sample		1951 census
Cohort born in	Total	% 'manual' (Cats. 4–7)	% 'manual' (R–G, 3–5)
1890–1899	540	78.7	78.4
1900–1909	751	79.7	79.2
1910–1919	772	83.1	81.5
1920–1929	755	89.0	87.7
Overall	3497	83.0	81.3

SOURCE: adapted from Glass, 1954, tables 1 and 12; 181 and 194.

It is Glass's argument that the smaller representation of older men in the 'manual' sector indicates a shift in the underlying occupational structure, towards the manual sector. In other words, the older men entered occupations when there were more 'non-manual' ones available – so fewer are in 'manual' occupations now – whereas the younger men were competing for a contracted supply of 'non-manual' jobs, and so were forced to appear in greater numbers as 'manual' employees.

A re-examination of the census data, this time including the three census points 1921, 1931 and 1951, and using approximately the same categorisation scheme shows the same general level of the dichotomy but its pattern over time for economically active males does not uphold Glass's position (see Table 6.6).

Table 6.6   Changes in proportions of 'manual' and 'non-manual' economically active men aged 20–64 in Scotland, England and Wales, 1921, 1931 and 1951

	'Manual' (SEG's 6–12, 15)			'Non-manual' (SEG's 1–5, 13, 14)			Totals (exluding armed forces, etc.)		
	England & Wales	Scotland	Combined	England & Wales	Scotland	Combined	England & Wales	Scotland	Combined
1921	86.8	86.2	86.7	13.2	13.8	13.3	11,744,964	1,480,834	13,255,798
1931	88.1	87.7	88.1	11.9	12.3	11.9	13,247,333	1,542,253	14,789,586
1951	84.8	85.1	84.8	15.2	14.9	15.2	13,419,178	1,540,784	14,959,962

SOURCE: Census Occupation tables.

These figures, taken direct from the censuses for three different time points, indicate that the 'manual' sector *fell by 2 per cent* between 1921 and 1951, despite the important fluctuation in 1931 due to the Depression, whereas Glass's figures, based on the cohorts of a single census, give the impression of a monotonic 9.3 per cent increase overall and 8.5 per cent for the three youngest cohorts. The use of the three census time points is more reliable than an estimate based on cohorts at a single time point. The findings from the three censuses match those of Bain *et al.* (1972) who, using a slightly different categorisation scheme on the occupational population of Britain, also report 1921 has a lower proportion of manual occupations than in 1931, but higher by around 2 per cent than in 1951. In addition, 1911 shows an even lower figure than for 1921, albeit by less than 1 per cent (Bain *et al.*, 1972, p. 113). Goldthorpe (1980a, p. 60) reports a contraction of 5 per cent, slightly more than does Routh (1965, pp. 4–5). Other writers on evidence of varying reliability have also supported the view that the long-term trend in industrial societies has been for a contraction of the manual sector, not the expansion Glass has claimed (see Chapter 4).

This interpretation is supported by the distribution of a sample of Scots born between 1910 and 1929. These men are the contemporaries of Glass's two youngest, 1910–19, and 1920–9 cohorts. While perfect correspondence is not to be expected (sampling error, national difference, coding compatibility), the direction of the difference between the two sets of figures, taken for caution's sake at a crude level, suggests that very similar men may be proportionately less 'manual' at a later stage in their careers. Sixteen per cent of the Glass 1910 cohort were in 'non-manual' jobs (categories 1–3, Glass, 1954, p. 186): interviewed in 1975 the Scottish 1910 cohort reported 23.6 per cent currently in 'non-manual' jobs. Glass's (younger) 1920 cohort were only 11.0 per cent 'non-manual' in 1949: 27.5 per cent of their Scottish contemporaries by 1975 were holding 'non-manual' jobs. It should be noted that overall, England and Wales has more non-manual occupations than Scotland. Therefore to find that it was the Scots in 1975 who were more non-manual than Glass's men suggests that 'career' maturity may have a considerable effect. If one accepts for a moment that both the Glass and the Scottish data on respondents themselves are reliable, then we are left with a career effect which helps to explain the difference between the reported levels of non-manual employment.

It is not unreasonable to suggest that age and hence intragenerational 'career' mobility takes sufficient men out of the manual sector through promotions to produce the cohort illusion which Glass takes for the real occupational structure. In other words, each successively younger cohort *is* more manual, but because *the men are younger*, and *not* because the occupational structure has changed.

Indeed Glass himself presents conflicting evidence. In a footnote discussing Bowley's work and updating it, he shows a small *increase* in 'non-manual' male occupations which he does not explain beyond reference to 'important elements of non-comparability' (Glass, 1954, p. 193). And while Glass also claims to find an expansion of the 'manual' sector for three groups each aged 45–54 in the 1911 to 1931 Census (Glass, 1954, pp. 191–2), this evidence is not only bedevilled by comparison problems, but confuses age equivalence with functional career equivalence. That is to say, entry to an occupational sector (such as foreman, or manager) is not always at an identical age for all men at all historical periods, even if entry into the non-manual sector always on average increases with age for any one cohort over time. This is because of institutional changes, such as educational reforms and the growth of credentialism, and historical events such as wars which affect men of different ages in different ways (for some, career prospects may be improved by the death of rivals or seniors, but in turn that accelerated group constitute a greater block to promotion for the next youngest cohort). The occupational situation of any cohort is the product of three major factors:

1. its unique historic location, which no other cohort can ever share;
2. its stage of career cycle, that is to say, its seniority, which other younger cohorts will in turn occupy; and
3. the changing occupational structures (with its expansion of non-manual opportunities) which applies to all cohorts, albeit more to the youngest cohort in the process of training and recruitment as this group is the most 'flexible'.

The interplay of these factors is complex, but Glass has interpreted the data on the three 45–54-year-old cohorts and the data in Table 6.4 above solely in terms of the last of these factors. He has mistaken what may be changes in access to certain jobs at different career stages for changes in the overall structure. By the same token, the evidence for the Scottish labour force quoted above must be regarded with caution because the increase in the non-manual proportion is not only due to seniority, as we implied, but is also due in part to changes of occupational structure. Although cohorts generally display little difference between their average status levels, this does not necessarily mean there is no career effect. It may be that older cohorts have benefited from career mobility, but that younger cohorts have benefited is proportionately more from the expansion of the non-manual sector, i.e. structural mobility. This kind of pattern therefore appears as the dominant one in current mobility studies which reflect the expansion of industrial society throughout this century (but see Hauser, 1975b, pp. 588–90, for a difference of emphasis).

ALTERNATIVE EXPLANATION OF GLASS'S RESULTS

Because of these observations about changes in the occupational structure, age effects, and differential fertility, Glass's interpretation of the problems apparent in his data cannot be accepted as a solution. The problems persist. Because gross mobility rates are necessarily dependent on the marginal distributions, *Social Mobility in Britain* provides an unreliable estimate of intergenerational occupational mobility, which in turn will require the revision of those of our theories of class relations in Britain which derive from the 1949 study.

If this is accepted, it is still an open question as to what went wrong with the LSE inquiry. The sample design is not obviously faulty, the response rate of 9296 out of 12,924 (75.9 per cent) is respectable and the age/marital status comparison with the Registrar-General's estimates suggest that the achieved interviews provided an adequate represent-ation of the population. Glass says that while there is some small bias in the age and marriage composition, it is doubtful if this is serious enough to affect the analysis, in part because the use of cohorts eliminates the overweighting of some age groups. The other variables –

> fertility and attainment of secondary education – do not appear to have been affected to any considerable extent . . . In sum, therefore, though the sample is by no means perfect, the bias involved is not likely to be crucial and is to a substantial extent counteracted by the method of analysis. (Glass, 1954, p. 92)

Indeed, as indicated below, the occupational representativeness of the respondents is not what is in question, since again, though not perfect, the bias is not great and it does not provide an explanation for the deviant fathers' distribution. By the same token, an overrepresentation of older age groups and married men does not explain the fathers' pattern. It would be an unfortunate chance if a sample which is unexceptional on five variables should be widely deviant on a sixth, which in turn we might expect to be related to at least some of the five.

A second possibility is a class differential in attrition rates: if migration and war casualties selected disproportionately for the sons of working-class fathers, then the residual population would appear to have an excess of middle-class fathers, because only the sons of the middle class would remain to be sampled. If this were a major effect, it would impinge most on the young men who fought the 1914–18 war, and who later participated in the great emigration of the late 1920s; that is to say, men born between 1890 and 1899. This cohort is only 75 per cent of the size of the other complete cohorts (Glass, 1954, p. 90), and so if there are significant differential attrition rates, this cohort should demon-strate them, assuming that some general process of adjustment has not since intervened.

In the first place, cohort 1890–9 does not show a marked excess of non-manual respondents, a necessary condition if its working-class population has suffered differential attrition. Its proportion is 21.3 per cent, only 0.9 per cent more than the next youngest generation. Second, although the cohort does have a higher proportion of non-manual fathers (20.6 per cent in categories 1, 2 and 3, while the others score 16.3 per cent, 17.4 per cent and 14.6 per cent in descending order of age) it is in line with the pre-1890 cohort which also has a high proportion, 21.6 per cent, but which has not been reduced in size by the war. Furthermore, the 1890–9 reduced cohort's net contribution to fathers is small precisely because it is a smaller cohort. Third, the marginal totals for the study mean that some downward mobility was almost inevitable – but within the differential attrition model, there is no immediate explanation of why the working-class sons of middle-class fathers were not equally at risk as working-class sons of working-class fathers – so sharply reducing the chances of the downwardly mobile of getting into Glass's sample. One is still left with the lack of fit between the fathers' and sons' distribution in a sample which adequately represents the population from which the *respondents* were drawn. Furthermore, another study only two years later (Benjamin, 1958, p. 266) reports 26.6 per cent non-manual fathers and 34.3 per cent non-manual sons (as against Glass's 37.1 per cent and 37 per cent).

It is, therefore, necessary to suggest that there is something seriously wrong with Glass's data, most probably in the father's occupations. The source of error may be something to do with the respondent's accuracy or veracity; it may lie in the interviewing technique; it may be a coding problem, or a combination of any of these. There is now no way to tell, because the interview schedules were destroyed as part of standard Civil Service procedures, and so are not available for analysis, although the discussion below reviews some further possibilities. But in the absence of some explanation which can *also* restore confidence in the data, it must be strongly urged that conclusions based on the mobility rates reported by Glass be held in abeyance.

This sceptical approach to the Glass data is not the position adopted by others writing since the father/son peculiarity became known. Perhaps it is the very recognition of the fact that the fathers' distribution does not represent a population in the normal sense that has discouraged them giving the matter further consideration. The international comparative sociologists (Bendix and Lipset, 1959; Miller, 1960; Svalstoga, 1965; Fox and Miller, 1966; Cutright, 1968; etc.) have all accepted Glass without question – as one would expect, given their general orientation towards grand comparative exercises and their lack of interest in cultural and historical variations, a common limitation of comparative analysis (Payne, 1973a). Bibby remarks on the similarity of the two generations, but uses the data as the cornerstone for his discussion of mobility measures (Bibby, 1975, p. 125). Duncan-Jones notes that 'it is well known that this table has rather a regular pattern' (Duncan-Jones, 1972, p. 195): again, he uses the data in his exposition (both Bibby and Duncan-Jones employ the Miller version of Table 6.3 (above) data (Miller, 1960)). It is slightly ironic that the development of the various coefficients and methods of analysis have used concrete examples drawn from a table that is so untypical of mobility tables generally.

Noble is one of the few commentators who has criticised the LSE study; however, despite doubts about the sample, he does not argue for the rejection of Glass's findings (Noble, 1972 and 1975a). He suggests that the 1949 study

> which is correctly indicating little change in occupational structure, but, simultaneously, over-representing non-manual workers among the respondents, may also seriously over-estimate the non-manual element in the generation their fathers represent. (Noble, 1972, p. 428)

In other words, he attributes the excess of non-manual fathers to an excess of non-manual sons in the sample. However, this involves a number of misinterpretations. First, Noble's statement is predicated on the assumption that Glass correctly indicates little occupational change, whereas the actual change, as indicated above, is very different from the picture Glass presents. Second, to what extent does Glass overrepresent the non-manual sons? Noble gives four different figures for the non-manual proportion in 1951: 26.4 per cent, 38.4 per cent, 32 per cent and 37 per cent. The first is for all males, the second is for household heads (both taken from the 1951 Census of Great Britain), the third is from Benjamin's study (Benjamin, 1958), and the fourth is Miller's classes 1 to 3a, taken from Miller's account (which despite Miller's claim, refers to England and Wales only). Noble uses the difference between the first and last of these figures as an indication that Glass's sample is unsatisfactory.

However, the correct comparison with the 37 per cent reported as non-manual sons by Glass is the age-adjusted English and Welsh civilian population figure for R–G's 1951 classes 1, 2 and 3, less the skilled workers, SEG 10: this gives 35.5 per cent as the census estimate, or an error of 1.5% (Census 1951, Occupation Tables, 148–49, Nos. 17 and 18). The earlier discussion of 'non-manual' by Glass gave the sample sons as 17 per cent 'non-manual' (Table 6.3 above, categories 1, 2 and 3), as against the census estimate of 18.1 per cent. So that while the sample is not perfect, its small error lies mainly in its shortage of upper middle class (categories 1, 2 and 3) and its excess of lower middle-class representation (category 4 and the routine white-collar part of category 5, which contribute to the 37 per cent figure). But the extent of the overrepresentation is not as great as Noble implies, and the larger part of it appears in the classes which are most open to imprecisions of coding.[4]

Even if there is an overrepresentation of non-manual sons, along the general lines of Noble's argument, this only relates to an excess of non-manual fathers provided that one accepts that there are high self-recruitment rates. But belief about these rates is of course largely based on Glass's work, so that an element of tautology creeps in. If we accept the figure of 1.5 per cent excess of non-manual sons, this appears to be equivalent to saying that about 54 cases in the first five categories of Miller's data should really be manual workers. But none of these could be removed from the top three categories because these are already in deficit (by about 1.1 per cent in the under 60s part of the sample) and indeed require an *addition* of, say, around 40 more non-manuals. The total effect is that the upper three non-manual categories (1 to 3) have 592 cases (17 per cent) and should have 633 (18.1 per cent), while the lower two non-manual categories 4 and 5a, have 703 (37–17 per cent) and should be 608 (35.5–18.1 per cent), for an overall non-manual total of 1241 (35.5 per cent). But if we assume that adjustment to non-manual sons changes the number of non-manual fathers by one for every son (i.e. assuming perfect self-recruitment at this dichotomous level), then while categories 4 and 5a would contribute fewer middle-class fathers, categories 1, 2 and 3 would contribute more; the 39 cases which are moved would 'take with them' their fathers, so that we would still have exactly the same excess of fathers, proportionate to the number of sons. If one assumes, more realistically, a more moderate degree of self-recruitment then the excess of non-manual fathers in class 1, 2 and 3 *increases* absolutely although not relatively, while the excess in 4 and 5a becomes relatively greater (since removing one son removes less than one father). Conversely the new replacement manual sons add less than their own number to the manual fathers, which worsens the shortage of manual fathers because the sons' total is increased more than the fathers'. This effect will be limited by the fact that there is less downward than upward mobility in industrial society, so that adding manual sons add mainly to the manual fathers whereas any adjustment to the non-manual sons has some effect on the manual fathers. Again, the impact of adjustment in one category depends on its size and pattern of recruitment. We are therefore unable to accept Noble's explanation of the discrepancies in the fathers and sons distributions.

Noble's original comments about errors in the sample develop from his view of age and career effects. He argues that household heads have a higher social class rating than 'all males' (26.4 per cent and 38.4 per cent non-manual in 1951), and because men with sons are more likely to be household heads, than 'all sons', there should be more fathers in the non-manual category than sons (Noble, 1972, p. 427). It is for this reason that he is less worried by the overrepresentation of non-manual fathers. However, since Glass is talking about men aged 20 or over, 'all sons' are closer to marriage age and household headship than 'all males', the latter including males 15–19. So if Noble is correct, 'all sons' should occupy the middle ground between household heads and 'all males'. It has already been shown that on the categories 1–5a definition, 35.5 per cent of 'sons' over 20 years old are non-manual; this compares with 36.0 per cent for all males and 37.0 per cent for household heads (Marsh, 1965, p. 200). (37.0 per cent is chosen in preference to Noble's 38.4 per cent in order that all three sets of figures are calculated in an identical way.) Thus, first, the difference between household heads and males is not as great as Noble suggests (1.5 per cent or at most 2.9 per cent on Noble's figure) and second, the 'all males' are *more* 'non-manual' than their older 'all sons', so suggesting that the age/household head effect is more complicated than it initially appears. Furthermore, an age effect on this scale would show up *if* the occupational structure was nearly stable, which contrary to Noble's view, it was not. So although he is aware of the peculiarities of the 1949 data, his assumptions about structural continuity and career effects prevent him from recognising the importance of the fathers' overrepresentation.

Similarly, while in a 1972 paper Ridge and Macdonald have commented on the way that the pre-dating fathers' distribution resembles the later sons' distribution (Ridge and Macdonald, 1972, p. 142), they continue to use the 1949 data in a search for mobility trends (and Ridge has carried out further analysis more recently; see p. 114). As they say, their tables for 1949 and 1951 (Benjamin, 1958), 1962 (Runciman, 1966), and 1963 (Butler and Stokes, 1969) show no clear patterns, and they hesitate to draw conclusions about trends from the evidence of those four tables. Having considered the lack of comparability due to different time points for the fathers' jobs, due to non-response, and the option of 'concocting a tale' to fit the discrepancies and finding in none of these solutions a satisfactory answer, they raise the possibility of eliminating one table. But because the criteria for selecting 'a table to discard are unclear' (Ridge and Macdonald, 1972, p. 142) they leave the question open. The implication of their elimination idea is that the Glass data-set is the odd-man-out: without it the sons' non-manual proportions would be 34.3 per cent, 35.6 per cent and 37.5 per cent for 1951, 1962 and 1963 respectively. The fathers' non-manual proportions would be 26.6 per cent, 25.6 per cent and 29.5 per cent (although this latter comparison is only approximate – see Ridge and Macdonald, 1972, pp. 142 and 146–7). These figures are closer to a consistent pattern and the three 'retained' time points all clearly showing the excess of non-manual sons over non-manual fathers. Thus whereas Ridge and Macdonald hesitate to discard the 1949 table for want of criteria, the present author would suggest that the evidence of this chapter provides sufficient grounds for the elimination of the LSE data to be made.

Graeme Ford (see Payne *et al.*, 1977) has identified further parallel peculiarities encountered by both Keith Hope (1975) and John Ridge (1974a) in their attempts to analyse the Glass data. In his paper 'Trends in the Openness of British Society in the Present Century' (1975) Hope explores changes in mobility by comparing the overlapping parts of the 1949 study and the 1972 Nuffield study. Even allowing for problems of replication, the two results do not match. First, the marginals are different, with the relevant part of the 1972 sample being much closer to the 1951 Census figures (Hope, 1975, Part II, Table 1). Second, the association between fathers and sons is weaker in the later survey: the product moment correlations being 0.47 in 1949 but 0.36 in the Oxford inquiry, a difference not explained just by the change in marginals. Hope concludes that to bring the two mobility tables into line would require a reduction in self-recruitment in all categories in the Glass study.

Hope goes on to explore possible reasons for the lack of fit, perhaps reflecting what was argued at the start of this chapter, that nobody wishes to doubt the credibility of Glass's study. He therefore examines differential effects of mortality and migration, and with reference to the Oxford sample, inaccurate recall, incorrect Hall-Jones coding, and poor interviewing. However, none of these, even had they been found to be applicable, explains why *self-recruitment* should be higher in 1949, or why the marginals should be different. Despite his apparent wish to retain the Glass evidence, Hope concludes that 'the two studies remain stubbornly divergent . . . it seems reasonable to place greater reliance on the results of the later enquiry rather than on those of the earlier study' (Hope, 1975, pp. 38 and 49).

The second source of discrepancies in the Glass data which Graeme Ford has identified is in the work of John Ridge (1974b). Ridge re-examines the correlations between the respondent, several brothers, and his father, and reports a number of unlikely outcomes. For example, instead of intersibling correlations being more or less equal, the 'between brother' value is higher than between the respondent and his brothers, while the respondent/father correlation is substantially higher than that between brothers and father.

Ridge explores various possible explanations such as sampling error, fallible memory, sample attenuation, and data processing error, without providing a satisfactory answer. He does, however, raise two speculations which deserve further consideration. The first is, quite simply, that respondents do not tell the truth. They downgrade their brothers out of 'sibling rivalry' and upgrade their fathers to their own achieved class position, as a result of neurotic status consciousness. This so undermines the whole enterprise of social mobility research as to be almost unthinkable! Happily, there are stronger grounds for refusing to countenance this possibility. If it were true, the excess of non-manual fathers in Glass (due to 'upgrading') would also appear in other mobility studies: as we have seen, there is no sign of this.

We could probably construct an explanation based on systematic distortion on the part of the respondents along the lines indicated above; the problem here is that it stands or falls on the imputation of complex motive and behaviour patterns which however superficially plausible, are unamenable to evidence. Furthermore, even if we are happy to take this course, we are left with one major question: exactly what was it about the Glass study that led to the respondents' falsifications, where other studies seem to show less evidence of such peculiarities?

The second problem which Ridge highlights is the actual recording and coding of the occupational data. The occupational information on brothers (and fathers) was collected in less detail than that for the respondent. In addition, as Macdonald (1974) and Hope and Goldthorpe (1974) have pointed out, the directions given to coders for applying the Hall-Jones scale were not comprehensive:

> the instructions followed in coding occupations into the Hall-Jones scale on the first occasion of its use [Glass, 1954] have never been published . . . Certainly it cannot be assumed, given the inadequate guidance under which coders must have worked, that highly comparable classifications of occupations have been produced. (Hope and Goldthorpe, 1974, pp. 7–8)

It is possible that the coding of the fathers' and brothers' occupations was less successful than for the respondent. This would not, however, explain why fathers were 'upgraded' and brothers 'downgraded', unless there was some additional factor which applied differentially to the fathers and brothers.[5] Coding error may lie at the back of the problem, but there is very little hard evidence to go on, and even so, there seems to be no parsimonious explanation for all of the various discrepancies that have been encountered.

CONCLUDING REMARKS ON GLASS

This chapter has not succeeded in locating a satisfactory answer of *why* the 1949 study produced dubious findings. However, it is the present author's contention that serious doubts have been raised about the results, most notably with respect to the fathers' occupational distribution and therefore by implication with respect to the flows of mobility reported. This was the central purpose of the chapter. As indicated at the beginning, and as we shall see in the following chapter, many sociologists have built models of the class structure on Glass's evidence, so that the critique of his work has far-reaching implications.

Nonetheless, it might be that the reader rejects the doubts outlined in the previous pages. If so, there is still good reason to hesitate in drawing too heavily on *Social Mobility in Britain* in anything other than a historical capacity: the Glass data refer to a very much earlier period, compared with the US or latest British studies.

Towards the upper limits, for the older respondents 1949, Glass was dealing with people whose birth year was in the early 1880s and whose fathers' birth year came in the mid-1840s (taking Glass's estimate of father's mid-child birth at age 34 (Glass, 1954, p. 191). Such a father would reach the equivalent of retirement age in 1910, still in the era of horse-drawn transport and well before the start of the First World War. His son could easily have worked for over 20 years before that war, and would be reaching retirement age during the Second World War. Of course, at the other end of the age scale, the 20-year-old born to a 34-year-old father had worked only since the end of that war, but his father's work experience would nevertheless start before the previous war – 1909. With successively older respondents, the father's work experience (particularly his entry into the labour force) becomes increasingly characterised by the interwar years, and the nineteenth century. It follows that the mobility Glass reports is strongly bound up in occupational and social processes that had little direct relevance in 1949. Over two-thirds of Glass's sample have their mobility defined by the occupations of fathers who reached retirement age before the end of the Second World War.

Thus the problem with *Social Mobility in Britain* can be seen as a much simpler and more obvious one. The research dates from 1949; we are now in the 1980s. Even in the peculiarly non-empirical traditions of British Sociology, normal practice would make sociologists hesitant in attributing to the social conditions of the 1960s, 1970s and 1980s the results of surveys carried out only four years after the end of the last war. But all mobility studies are by nature retrospective and historical, and the LSE study is now more historical than most. It follows that there can be very little justification in uncritically regarding the present mobility processes of Britain (or 'advanced industrial society') as being those reported by Glass, something which certainly was the practice until very recently.

Nonetheless, it would be ungenerous in the extreme to finish this chapter without paying tribute to David Glass. Despite all of the criticisms outlined above, his contribution to the field of social mobility as an original thinker and as a stimulus to other scholars was nothing short of monumental. And at a much lower and personal level, he was helpful and courteous in the extreme to the present author when the early work for this chapter was being carried out. It is only possible to operate in the field of social mobility at its current level because of the groundwork which he did.

7   The New Account of Mobility

If the evidence of Glass's work is to be rejected, and with it many of the conclusions based upon it, the main alternative sources of data are the national mobility studies carried out in the 1970s. These are the Oxford studies of England and Wales, in particular what is probably the best known account produced by John Goldthorpe (1980a), and the Scottish Mobility Study, directed by the author. These studies are not without their own problems. The choice of classification and indices, the balance of the commentary on the data, and the conceptual perspectives, are all open to varying degrees of criticism. However, rather than leaving a vacuum, it is better to compare some of the features of the two studies, and to present some illustrations from the Scottish Mobility Study to show how an occupational approach throws a new light on mobility (a much fuller account is to be found in Payne, 1986).

THE OXFORD STUDY

Despite its greater technical sophistication and conceptual development, the Oxford study is very much in the Glass tradition, although its results, and the way these are presented, are somewhat different. What is interesting about these results in the present context is not so much the actual rates of mobility as the choice of measures and the way the reader's interpretation of these is coloured by the commentary.

We have already seen that in the Oxford data there are more non-manual sons than fathers (56 per cent and 46 per cent, see Goldthorpe, 1980a, Table 2.1, p. 44). Clearly, the expansion of the non-manual sector has benefits for sons from both manual and non-manual families. Roughly a quarter of the sample had been upwardly mobile whereas a third had been born non-manual and remained so. Compared with early assumptions based on Glass, these are very different results, although of course they are very far from indicating an open society. The same point can be made for mobility into Goldthorpe's service class. Goldthorpe's class I is twice the size of Glass's classes I and II, but expressed as an inflow we have 28 per cent of Goldthorpe's top class being recruited from manual families – rather more than we would have expected from Glass's account, in which the inflow to classes I and II combined is only about 19 per cent. These snapshots of the total process, together with the overall percentage of men who were upwardly mobile by at least one class, which is 43 per cent, suggest a society which has substantial fluidity.

Goldthorpe, on the other hand, tends to present an account which does not pay attention to this fluidity, but to the extent of closedness in modern Britain. For example, he talks more about the relative mobility findings, that is to say the comparison of chances of people from different origins reaching a desirable destination, and indeed in places discusses these net of any structural effects. This discussion is certainly intrinsically interesting, and further the *paradox* of having absolute mobility increase but relative mobility stagnate, is an eye-catching result. Nonetheless, it is essentially a pessimistic view which leads the reader towards seeing British society as more closed and thereby more *static* than is necessary. After all, ordinary people *perceive* mobility as happening or not happening, they do not *experience* mobility in terms of the relative chances of different origin groups entering various destinations.

We can consider the chances of, say, one hundred men of experiencing mobility as a *family* phenomenon. Of these one hundred sons, 43 will be upwardly mobile by at least one of Goldthorpe's seven classes. The remaining 57 will have their own children – or more accurately, about 80 per cent of them will – so that about 46 will have sons. If 43 per cent of these 46 will, on average, be upwardly mobile, that is 20 of them. So in total, about 63 will either be mobile themselves or have sons who have 'got on in life'. Only about one-third of families will not have experienced upward mobility on the part of one member. And some of this one-third will already be so high in the class hierarchy that there is really nowhere higher to be mobile to.

This rule of thumb calculation suggests a society in which there is considerable fluidity; certainly sufficient fluidity to require of us as sociologists that we come to terms with it. Goldthorpe directs our attention away from it, in part because of the narrow view of his subject, derived from his political position, and part because he underestimates the significance of the key process in mobility, namely occupational transition.

We have already observed the way in which Goldthorpe attempts to place mobility analysis in Marxist writing. In his first chapter of *Social Mobility and Class Structure in Modern Britain*, he takes to task commentators who have argued that the study of social mobility is an exercise in bourgeois apologia. His account of earlier contributions to the study of mobility seeks to identify the various authors' 'interests'. He writes:

> There is no *necessary* connection between a research interest in mobility and any specific ideological attachment . . . On the other hand, though, we would recognise, and insist upon the need to recognise, that mobility research is an ideologically loaded area – in the sense underlying a research interest in it, one must expect there to be also an interest of a different kind, which in some ways derives from the researcher's own socio-political experience, values, and commitments. (Goldthorpe, 1980a, p. 2)

Goldthorpe describes his own ideological position or interest as 'the implications for class formation and class action' which social mobility has, that is, drawing on a 'marxian or at least *marxisant*' tradition (1980, p. 28). This means that by showing how far short of a genuinely open society we have, the ideal of the open society and the need for 'collective action on the part of those in inferior positions' (1980a, p. 29) can be restated. His emphasis on relative mobility and outflow measures relates directly to this concern.

Goldthorpe is also very much concerned to develop his own ideas on social class. Because he is promoting a relatively new idea in the 'service class', he tends to emphasise those parts of his data which relate to the service class more than the other classes and their inter-movement. This is not to suggest that he does not present all of the relevant data, but rather that these get left buried in the tables. Thus, for example, in Chapter 2, where Goldthorpe discusses the buffer zone thesis, counter-mobility, occupational change and basic mobility patterns, classes I and II, the senior and junior elements of the service class, are mentioned roughly five times for every mention of a movement or non-movement in the other five classes. There is no inherent reason why classes I and II should receive more attention (given that this excludes the section on the closure thesis where justifiably there should be more talk of classes I and II), except in terms of Goldthorpe's interpretative framework. Indeed, one might even share his sense of priorities. But it does mean that any percentages of mobility flow that readers may recall, having had their attention drawn to them, will be for only part of the total mobility pattern.

Does this matter? It does, for two reasons. First, among the classes that are under-represented in his commentary is that containing super-visors, technicians and small businessmen. In the Scottish Mobility

Study data, using slightly different classification, this 'class' is not noticeably bigger than the other non-manual classes but it contributes at least one-third of all upward mobility. In other words, if we are to get a clear picture of upward mobility we need to pay attention to precisely those categories which Goldthorpe tends to underplay in his commentary.

A second reason why Goldthorpe's treatment matters, lies in his conceptualisation of the class structure. He explicitly states that he is unsure how the classes III, IV and V fit into the class hierarchy so he cannot be sure if movements in and out of these are upward or downward mobility. But this reflects his idiosyncratic definitions of classes which as Penn (1981) has shown, owe little to the Hope–Goldthorpe scale, or to classical class theory. It is no wonder that, if Goldthorpe is unclear about the class structure, his picture of mobility (and the one he offers us) is itself at times unclear. Goldthorpe also tends to underplay the extent of mobility in his discussion of occupational change and relative mobility. Although he does acknowledge the extent of occupational transition, this is a relatively late addition to his thinking. In an earlier draft of Chapter 2, given at a symposium at Aberdeen University in 1975, there was no mention of this structural change. In his book, there is a brief four-page discussion of the extent of occupation transition, but more typical is his conclusion to the log linear modelling account in Chapter 4. First he reports the positive side:

> the chances of men of all orgins including working class ones to acceed to higher level class positions have steadily increased over recent decades in absolute terms; and during this period the heterogeneity of social origins of those holding such position has in consequence surely grown. (Goldthorpe, 1980a, p. 114)

He then immediately proceeds to balance this by writing:

> nonetheless, these developments are not only consistent with a situation of no change in relative mobility chances . . . but further, with a situation in which the inequalities of such chances that prevail are ones of a quite gross kind, at least as between the higher division of the service class and the working class. It is here it may be said, that the reality of contemporary British society most strikingly and incontrovertibly deviates from the ideal of genuine openness. (Goldthorpe, 1980a, p. 114)

This is not to say that Goldthorpe is wrong, but rather that he is concentrating on the negative side of his results. If one looks at absolute mobility, that is, the number of men who are upwardly mobile in simple terms, or at inflow measures, that is to say the number of people in a class who have come from different origins, we find a different impression. Because Goldthorpe is wedded to a concern with mobility as part of stratification in a narrow sense, rather than seeing it as a part of a less ideologically loaded area like occupation, both he and his reader find their attentions focused on the absence of openness in British society, rather than the considerable levels of fluidity which exist, despite the class structure.

ALTERNATIVE EVIDENCE OF ABSOLUTE AND INFLOW MOBILITY

The Scottish data provide two kinds of information: more or less conventional evidence about mobility (albeit in a presentation influenced by a concern with the occupational dimensions) and a new kind of evidence expressed in historical and situational terms. The first of these will act as a bridge between old and new. Table 7.1, shows male mobility between the respondent's job at the time of interview, and his father's job when the respondent was 14 years old. That is to say, it follows the Oxford conventions in all respects, except that the seven classes are different.

The first observation to make is that the marginal distributions (the row and column totals) show a structural shift between the generations, with the three manual classes (V, VI and VII) having more fathers, whereas the 'non-manual' classes (strictly speaking, these include some technicians and self-employed craftsmen with high Hope–Goldthorpe scale scores) show the reverse. The largest expansion is in the professional/managerial group, the largest contraction is in the skilled manual group.

If we total the cells below, on, and above the main diagonal from top left to bottom right, Table 7.1 shows that 42.3 per cent of the sample were upwardly mobile by at least one category, 27.4 per cent were immobile (9.8 per cent in the non-manual class and 17.5 per cent manual), and 30.3 per cent were downwardly mobile. In other words, on the basis of these gross mobility rates, about three in every four men experience some kind of disjunction between their family background and their own occupational identity (forgetting for the moment any additional respondents whose earlier career took them away from their origins before they returned to the same category at the time of interview). This suggests a relatively fluid condition.

Table 7.1 Intergenerational male mobility (numbers=absolute mobility, percentages are inflows)

	Father's occupation when respondent aged 14	Respondent's occupation at time of interview							
		I	II	III	IV	V	VI	VII	Totals
I	Professionals; managers; senior administrators	128 (23.3)	71 (10.3)	18 (2.8)	29 (10.9)	14 (1.4)	14 (1.6)	12 (1.8)	286
II	Semi-professionals; white-collar supervisors	108 (19.6)	193 (28.0)	62 (9.6)	45 (16.9)	54 (5.8)	72 (8.0)	35 (5.3)	569
III	Foremen; self-employed artisans	76 (13.8)	95 (13.8)	121 (18.8)	26 (9.7)	91 (9.7)	110 (12.2)	75 (11.4)	594
IV	Routine white collar	41 (7.5)	35 (5.1)	16 (2.5)	15 (5.6)	21 (2.2)	14 (1.6)	11 (1.7)	153
V	Skilled manual	91 (16.5)	128 (18.6)	172 (26.7)	63 (23.6)	400 (42.6)	265 (29.5)	217 (32.9)	1336
VI	Semi-skilled manual	51 (9.3)	92 (13.4)	131 (20.3)	47 (17.6)	193 (20.6)	257 (28.6)	152 (23.0)	923
VII	Unskilled manual	55 (10.0)	75 (10.9)	124 (19.3)	42 (15.7)	166 (17.7)	167 (18.6)	158 (23.9)	787
	Totals	550 (100)	689 (100)	644 (100)	267 (100)	939 (100)	899 (100)	660 (100)	4648

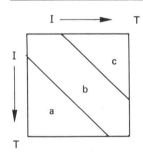

Absolute mobility	%
a=upwardly mobile	=42.3
b=immobile	=27.4
c=downwardly mobile	=30.3

Of course, had we used a smaller number of categories, such as 'manual' and 'non-manual', the appearance of the results would be different. In this case, 23 per cent of the sample were upwardly mobile, 65.7 per cent were immobile and 11.3 per cent were downwardly mobile. We might hesitate to call this 'fluid', but this still shows one in three men being mobile. Conversely, if we were to operate exclusively with the 20 categories which were used for parts of the analysis, the upward mobility figure would be 51 per cent and the downward 34 per cent. Thus the selection of a seven-category model of the occupational order directly influences both the detail of the findings and also the way the reader interprets the level of mobility.

Part of this mobility can be attributed in a direct way to the changes in the occupational distributions between the two generations. This is shown in Table 7.2, which also includes immobility and downward mobility. Two-thirds of the upward mobility is concentrated in the three upper classes which consist of just over one-third of the sample. No other class has substantially more mobility than its 'proportional share'; contracting classes have less upward mobility than their proportional share. None of the classes except V deviates much from its proportional 'share' when it comes to immobility. Classes II and III have a relatively low share of downward mobility, whereas classes IV, VI and particularly VII are sites for disproportionately high levels of downward mobility; some kind of 'ceiling' and 'floor' effect may be present in these numbers. Even so, in considering the mobility characteristics of the various occupational groups, Table 7.2 helps to identify that the profiles are quite distinct, and generally compatible with an explanation that draws on occupational transition (there is no arithmetic reason why the pattern should be this neat).

Table 7.2 Proportions of mobility associated with classes

	Expanding occupations*				Contracting occupations			
	1	2	3	4	5	6	7	Totals
% of all upmobility	21.4	21.6	22.5	7.7	18.2	8.5	n.a.	100 (1968)
% of all immobility	10.1	15.7	9.5	1.2	31.5	20.2	12.4	100 (1272)
% of all downmobility	n.a.	5.0	5.7	7.1	12.8	33.7	35.7	100 (1408)
% of sample	11.8	14.8	13.9	5.7	20.2	19.3	14.2	100 (4648)

*'Expanding' and 'contracting' both as shown in the sample data and in terms of changes in the Registrar-General's socio-economic groups (Payne, 1977a).

However, one would not expect these data to show exact correspondence between occupational size and mobility because the 'occupational' approach is not one that deals only in changes in size. It also includes ideas about other facets of occupational change, such as changing standards of recruitment, or shortages of labour supply, or unemployment. The changing occupational distributions are the framework within which these 'rules' and others less directly to do with labour, like access to schooling, operate. Occupational transition is neither a simple, nor a monocausal, explanation of mobility.

The inflow percentages in Table 7.1 show the wide range of origins from which the present members of each class have come. Thus clearly class I is not a closed category. Three out of every four of its members have come from other origins, one in three from manual backgrounds, and each of the manual categories contributes about 10 per cent or more, even if its largest source of recruitment is from itself, followed by the adjacent class II. This is one of the more significant findings, because it shows that 'long range' mobility, from low in the hierarchy of backgrounds to a much higher ranked occupation, is not only possible but does indeed happen.

In contrast, while class II (consisting mainly of semi-professionals and technical workers with high levels of skills, plus managers and owners of small enterprises) also recruits from a wide range of origins, it shows the highest degree of self-recruitment of any non-manual class. This is due in part to the component categories (not shown in Table 7.1) which include farmers and small businessmen, the two occupational groups with exceptionally high self-recruitment – presumably due to the key role of property inheritance. Among present-day farmers, 56 out of 84 (67 per cent) were born the sons of farming fathers, while 41 out of 146 (32 per cent) small proprietors came from a small business background. Among the semi-professionals and technical workers who make up the rest of the class, the self-recruitment figure is only 5.2 per cent.

Class III consists of foremen and self-employed craftsmen, i.e. those occupational roles which have a commonsense career connection to skilled manual employment. The high proportion of mobility actually found in this class can be explained, not just be class expansion, but by structural connection of career significance to the manual worker. The system offers a space for the one-man operation in the interstices between large-scale production, which can occasionally allow an individual to graduate from being a manual worker to being a proprietor of some significance. It seems likely, however, that such a development may be more important to capitalism as a pacifying and legitimising myth for the working class than as a new source of entrepreneurial dynamism.

Class IV, routine white-collar work, is here the smallest (because many such workers are female) and has a recruitment pattern more in line with the non-manual sector than the manual. It recruits less than its 'share' from manual backgrounds, i.e. on the expectations of no association, and more from the non-manual. However, it has an unusually low rate of self-recruitment, only 5.6 per cent (the next lowest is class III with 18.8 per cent) and its recruitment from all classes is very close to the appropriate proportions.

In contrast to the routine white-collar category, skilled manual workers are both the largest class and the most self-recruited. This is a contracting class, like farming and small businesses; 1336 sons came from skilled manual families, but there were only 939 niches for them. The 'natural' connection with class III accounts for 172 of them, while 42.6 per cent of the present skilled workers are self-recruited. This may reflect an ability to pass on limited occupational advantage (*vis-à-vis* the rest of the manual labour force) to the next generation, by means of manipulating the apprenticeship scheme. It is not conventional to conceive of this kind of self-recruitment as self-interested closure – in the way that elite recruitment is normally treated. Nonetheless, the basic principle would seem to be operating at a secondary level lower down the scale.

What is evident is that class V is substantially the largest in both generations and other things being equal, would be expected to have prominent interactions with all other classes as a source of their recruits. However, the converse does not hold true. Table 7.1 shows that less than 2 per cent of the skilled category come from class I (a pattern shared with the other two manual classes). In all, about four out of every five skilled workers comes from a manual background; again, a pattern common to all manual classes.

The semi-skilled, and the unskilled, manual classes resemble each other, and indeed the decisions to call one job semi-skilled rather than unskilled was sometimes hard to justify. The main difference in inflow is that each recruits more heavily from among its own sons than from the other. Both are also contracting sectors, although the contraction of the semi-skilled category is somewhat less marked. Neither recruit as much as 2 per cent from class I, and only around one in five of their numbers come from non-manual backgrounds.

The central point about Table 7.1 is the high level of movement, a much higher level than one would expect from most sociological writing in Britain. Within the *system* of occupational stratification, there is considerable *individual* mobility. If we regard mobility as one index of the rigidity of that system, then it is necessary to modify our conception of mobility in Britain (or strictly speaking, Scotland).

The second general point to be made on the basis of Table 7.1 concerns class formation and the generation of class consciousness. Occupational mobility tends to result in people experiencing different life-styles: one in their families of origin and one – or more – in their own adult careers. It may be that an intergenerational shift between two adjacent categories of the seven-category scheme is unimportant in this context, but a move from one end of the scale to the other clearly is. The mobility data on the present middle class suggest that any notions of social homeogeneity and shared values which draw on what is brought to the current class situation from family of origin, might be suspect. It is not possible to entertain ideas of a non-manual class developing as a class 'for itself' when its collective experience is restricted to much less than a single lifetime. With heavy recruitment from the manual sector, the non-manual class may wish to stress its difference from and superiority over manual workers – but that is a far more dynamic and at the same time constrained situation, than one in which successive generations of a class are overwhelmingly self-recruited.

However, this situation is less true for the working class. Although there is some downward mobility, the main pattern is that manual workers are the sons of the previous generation of manual workers. There is considerable interchange between the levels of manual work (skilled/semi-skilled/unskilled) between generations and this may provide some kind of heterogeneity of life experience in the way that we have seen for the middle class. It certainly is not provided by the inflow of sons from above, and manual workers have more basis for a common identity and consciousness than do non-manual workers.

The continuity of working-class membership is also well illustrated by the patterns of outflow from manual class origins, although outflow analysis can be misleading at first sight because the percentages are more constrained by the size of the destination categories. Thus for example, the small values in the class IV column say more about the fact that there are only 5.7 per cent of all occupations in that category, rather than any process of connection between white-collar work and other origins. It is not proposed to explore Table 7.3 in the same detail as Table 7.1, but certain features do stand out.

Despite the earlier emphasis placed on movements between occupations the children of both the higher classes – and particularly class I – have a much better chance of good jobs than other children. Only about 14 per cent of the sons of managers and professionals and 28.4 per cent of the sons of semi-professionals ended up in manual work. In contrast, roughly 65 per cent of manual workers' sons became manual workers, i.e. in absolute terms they were four times more likely, and man for man twice as likely, to be manual workers than the sons of professionals. Nearly half of those born into class I held their position and another quarter ended up in the adjacent class II. Less than one in every fourteen sons of manual workers made it to the upper middle class.

Table 7.3 Intergenerational outflow mobility

| | Respondents' occupational class at time of interview | | | | | | | |
	I	II	III	IV	V	VI	VII	Totals
I	44.8	24.8	6.3	10.1	4.9	4.9	4.2	100 (286)
II	19.0	33.9	10.9	7.9	9.5	12.7	6.2	100 (569)
III	12.8	16.0	20.4	4.4	15.3	18.5	12.6	100 (594)
IV	26.8	22.9	10.5	9.8	13.7	9.2	7.2	100 (153)
V	6.8	9.6	12.9	4.7	29.9	19.8	16.2	100 (1336)
VI	5.5	10.0	14.2	5.1	20.9	27.8	16.5	100 (923)
VII	7.0	9.5	15.8	5.3	21.1	21.2	20.1	100 (787)
Totals	11.8	14.8	13.9	5.7	20.2	19.3	14.2	4648

Father's occupational class when respondent was aged 14

This comparison of chances shows the advantage which birth brings. The Fabian and radical themes discussed in earlier chapters pointed to the importance of any deviation from equality of opportunity. However, the basic structure of occupational opportunity must not be neglected: the immobility of many of the sons of manual workers can be seen as being that part of the outcome which would be expected if there was no parental advantage involved. Thus if, say, skilled work is about 20 per cent of employment then about 20 per cent of the sons of each class would be in skilled manual work – including the sons of skilled manual workers. In fact, the latter's proportion is about 30 per cent, an 'overload' of 10 per cent. But the flow from both semi-skilled and unskilled manual origins into skilled work is 'about right', while those from the non-manual classes are low. Given the earlier observations about self-recruitment in contracting classes like skilled manual work, it is interesting to speculate whether these patterns represent some kind of excessive self-recruitment or the outcome of a blockage preventing a distinct proportion of able-skilled manual workers' sons from entering the non-manual class.

In leaving the discussion of outflow rates here, it is worth reiterating the point that selection of measures and emphasis in commentary has a strong effect on reader perception. Because the present account is concerned less with class and more with occupational movements, there is no ideological reason to stress how closed is the opportunity structure of capitalism. It follows that absolute and inflow mobility rates have been given much more prominence than in other accounts, such as that of Goldthorpe. It is not the author's contention that Britain is an open society but rather that a fuller appreciation of the extent of occupational fluidity is essential to a proper analysis of contemporary class structures.

MODELS OF MOBILITY AND THE BRITISH CLASS STRUCTURE

The simplest model of class and mobility proposes a mobility 'threshold' at the manual/non-manual boundary. Westergaard and Resler (1977), who ironically have done much to restore social mobility to the centre of the stratification debate by the attention they give it in *Class in a Capitalist Society*, claim that there is a

> persistence of some mobility threshold along the line dividing manual from non-manual labour, even if it is lower than before . . . That line in fact has something of the character of a barrier against mobility. (Westergaard and Resler, 1977, pp. 302 and 301)

In the first place, as has already been shown, about one-third of the sample moved across that line in one direction or the other. This does not seem like a serious mobility hurdle. Second, within each of the four non-manual classes, there is considerable recruitment from the other side of the threshold: 35.8, 42.9, 66.3 and 56.9 per cent respectively. The reverse is less clear-cut: the three manual classes recruit 19.2, 23.4 and 20.2 per cent from the non-manual sector, about one in every five. Third, if the manual/non-manual line is to be regarded as a key hurdle, it should presumably be a more formidable obstacle than exists elsewhere in the occupational structure, i.e. the mobility flow across it should be lower than between any other two points in the mobility table. So for example, it should be harder to move from manual to non-manual, than from 'semi- and un-skilled' into 'skilled and non-manual' occupations. But whereas the former has a mobility flow of 34.3 per cent, the latter is only 38.7 per cent and again the flow between the sector comprising classes I, II and III, and that comprising IV, V, VI and VII, is 34.2 per cent. In other words, moving the threshold up or down one category does not seriously change the mobility flow.

We can extend this analysis by using the outflow rates in Table 7.3.

Each of the three manual classes exports more than one-third of its sons into non-manual occupations, which is less than would be expected on a no-association assumption (when one would look for nearer half of such sons to be in non-manual work), but still is a considerable flow. The counter flow is slightly smaller for classes II and IV, bigger for class III, and only about one in seven from class I. The idea of the threshold does not receive sufficient support from these data to be accepted. Perhaps a semi-permeable membrane might be a better analogy.

The second model which has been advanced as representing the main features of mobility in Parkin's 'Buffer Zone'. In this model

> The children of manual workers who cross the class line tend to assume fairly modest white-collar positions – as clerks, salesmen, shop assistants, schoolteachers, and the like. Recruitment to the established middle class professions requiring long periods of training and education is far less common . . . We could sum up these remarks by suggesting that there is what might be called a social and cultural 'buffer zone' between the middle class and working class proper. Most mobility, being of a fairly narrow social span, involves the movement into and out of this zone rather than movement between the class extremes. (Parkin, 1971, pp. 51 and 56)

The effect of this buffer zone is to insulate the 'middle class proper' from the culturally disruptive incursions of large numbers of ex-working class incomers, so securing the middle class's privilege and also maintaining class values and identity. In the seven-category classification, the buffer zone can be equated with classes III and IV, and the dominant pattern of movement should therefore be between these two and classes I and II, or classes V, VI and VII. If we examine inflows (Table 7.1) to classes I and II, there is on the contrary a larger flow direct from classes V, VI and VII than from classes III and IV, in fact, almost exactly double (39.7 per cent of the total, compared with 19.9 per cent). However, the flow into the two intermediate classes from below is heavier than the flow from classes V, VI and VII into the upper two categories: 579 cases compared with 492. A strict test of the buffer zone model would have to be that not only was this latter condition fulfilled, but the intermediate-to-upper flow would also have to be greater than the manual-to-upper flow, which it is not.

Parkin does not say much about the function of the buffer zone in *downward* mobility. Here the picture is the reverse of the upward pattern, with a smaller direct flow from classes I and II to the manual classes than that from the intermediate classes, but with a larger direct flow than that into the buffer zone. Again, only one of the two required conditions is met. Even if one takes the outflow figures, the model cannot be clearly substantiated. The percentage flows direct into classes I and II from the manual classes are 3 per cent greater than those into the buffer zone classes. The downward flows from class I direct to manual occupations are slightly smaller than to the intermediate zone (14.0 per cent as compared with 16.4 per cent) but those from class II are much larger (28.4 per cent and 18.8 per cent).

The heart of the problem for the buffer zone model is its more general assumption that all mobility is predominantly over a short range. If Parkin were correct, each class should have intakes which consist mainly of recruits from the immediately adjacent categories. But if the immobile are discounted, then all but one of the categories draw only around one-third of their remaining intake from the categories immediately shown above and below them: the notable exception is the semi-skilled group with double this level of 'local' recruitment, which may in part be due to technical problems of deciding the limits of semi-skilled occupations. Intergenerational mobility does not predominantly consist of a series of one-place, short-range steps, from one category to the next: recruitment draws instead from a wide spectrum of origins, although as was noted above, manual occupations have higher levels of mutual intake.

Among current manual workers, only one in five has been mobile over a 'long distance' which includes crossing the manual/non-manual line. Conversely, the non-manual sector consists of 25 per cent of the total workforce which is interrecruited, with an equal amount added from manual origins: one in two is a long-distance mobile in this half, so that the heterogeneity of the non-manual sector is far greater than in the manual. Thus while Parkin may be correct in saying that not many semi-skilled or unskilled workers are recruited from the sons of professionals, managers and so on (but still nearly 1 in 10 in this case), 36 per cent of the present category I, and 43 per cent of category II come from the other side of the buffer zone.

It may be that the mobility over two generations and the intermediate classes does serve the functions which Parkin proposes, but it is not the dominant pattern of mobility. Such a process might be better pictured as a kind of fairly effective safety net, or perhaps a non-return valve, against downward mobility rather than a filter against upward mobility. This would be to change the significance which Parkin attaches to the buffer zone analogy very substantially, and to stress protection for offspring rather than closure against incomers.

The final model of mobility is the one to be found in Bottomore (1965) and Miliband (1969), that upward movement becomes progressively less, the further up the class hierarchy. This model also draws on the idea of short-range mobility, but it additionally confuses access to elites with access to the upper middle class of professionals and managers. Several studies, such as Stanworth and Giddens (1974) have shown elite self-recruitment figures as high as 80 per cent, but both the Oxford and the Scottish studies show self-recruitment to their respective classes I more in the region of 25 per cent. There is a marked discontinuity between the general category of professionals and managers, and those key posts such as cabinet ministers, senior civil servants, directors of major companies, editors and senior people in the media. The mobility data are available from Table 7.1, and a more detailed consideration of this argument can be found elsewhere (see for example, Payne and Ford, 1977a and b, Payne, 1986). The present cursory treatment of elite recruitment does not mean that the argument is unimportant, but there is insufficient space to develop it here, given that parallels have already been reported for the Oxford mobility data.

HISTORICAL TRENDS IN OCCUPATIONS AND MOBILITY

Much of the previous section does not depend on the occupational approach developed earlier in the book, although the use of absolute and inflow measures in presenting data to replace the vacuum left by Glass does. It also provides both replication and an alternative view of the Oxford study. However, we can now extend the occupational treatment by looking at trends and industrial sectors.

The measures of mobility used will be intergenerational mobility, across the manual/non-manual line, to the respondent's first job. In other words, we are using the common but somewhat crude level of a dichotomy, but restricting the extent of mobility to initial entry into the labour force. This enables us to control for career development, because the older men in the sample would otherwise have had more time in which to be mobile than the younger men. This improves the picture of trends, but omits the full scale of mobility, and therefore it must be remembered that the argument presented refers to the mobility of young men just starting work. A parallel analysis of jobs ten years after starting work, but not presented here, shows a nearly parallel profile to that of first job, except of course that ten years more mobility has taken place: differences in starting work persist well into later careers. Because we wish to retain the possibility of connections to real events, the trend analysis has been based on year of entry to the labour market, rather than on conventional year of birth cohorts. This enables us to talk more directly about the state of the occupational structure at any one time, because the data then refer to all starting work, whether aged 14 or 24. Although men born in the same year share certain experiences (e.g. education) they do not all start work at the same time and under the same economic conditions. In practice the following analysis therefore refers to men who were first employed between 1930 and 1970, because before this only the men in the sample without post minimum school leaving age education were entering work (and so more likely to take manual jobs), while after 1970 the entrants would all have post minimum school leaving age education (and therefore be disproportionately manual).

A second methodological departure is to abandon the use of fixed cohorts. Conventionally, trend analysis of mobility uses fixed cohorts, starting with the year of birth of the oldest respondent and reckoning ten-year block forward to the present, from that date. Thus Glass's cohorts run 1890–9, 1900–9, 1910–19 and 1920–9, while Goldthorpe's are 1908–17, 1918–27, 1928–37 and 1938–47. One difficulty with this is that these dates are determined by the year of the survey, rather than by an interest in a period of historical events. Therefore the cohorts may straddle countervailing trends and disguise chronological patterns (the cohorts have to be ten years long to retain large numbers for analysis). One way around this is to use 'rolling cohorts', i.e. moving averages based on successive, partially overlapping, groups of years. Instead of a table showing four cohorts, the data are presented as lines on a graph.

When looking at the graphs it is important to remember that the five-year cohort is plotted at its mid-point: thus 1930–4 is plotted as 1932. The change between two adjacent points reflects the net effect of dropping out the oldest year and introducing a new one (1930–4 becomes 1931–5) so it is important to look on either side of the points to see the period in question. It may also be worthwhile to make the cautionary note that it is wise to remember that trend analysis, particularly when it compares changes between the beginning and end of a 40-year period, or periods encompassing dramatic changes, needs to be treated with caution.

Figure 7.1 shows the pattern of changes in occupational distribution and in mobility for men entering the labour market from 1930 through to the late 1960s. Allowing for an odd kink here and there, the upper line shows a decade of expansion of non-manual occupations, from an origin around 18 per cent. This was followed by a decade of contraction, but the fall was not to the former levels. Finally, men starting work from about 1950 on did so during a considerable expansion of non-manual work, rising to a point in excess of 40 per cent.

Figure 7.1 Five-year moving averages for non-manual employment and mobility on first entry to labour market

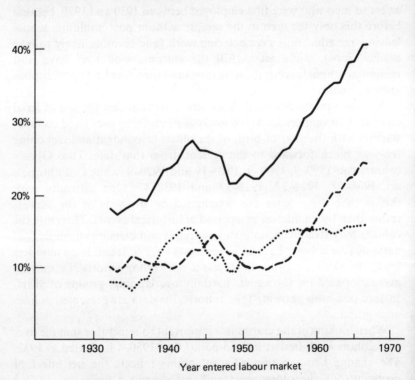

Year entered labour market

——— % Non-manual first employment
······ % Non-manual first employment and recruited from *manual* family
– – – % Non-manual first employment and recruited from *non-manual* family

If we examine the lower line, showing the percentage of upward mobility from manual backgrounds to non-manual employment, the first part of the pattern echoes the occupational distribution line, with a decade of increase followed by a decade of decrease. However, although mobility begins to increase in the 1950s, it levels off at around 15 per cent by the mid or late 1950s. This is double its earlier level, but the apparent association of mobility and opportunity disappears.

Instead, the expansion of non-manual occupations is filled by men from non-manual backgrounds. This is shown by the middle, dotted, line which hovers between 10 and 15 per cent until the late 1950s but then takes off at a similar rate to the expansion of non-manual employment line. In short, as far as mobility across the manual/non-manual line at the first job is concerned, the upward mobility rate has ceased to improve. Indeed, in the last decade of the period covered by the Scottish Mobility Study, it has worsened *vis-à-vis* the rate at which the sons of the non-manual class gain access to non-manual work themselves.

Both the proportions of non-manual and upwardly mobile rise between 1930–4 and 1941–5, the rise being more marked from 1936–40 on as the war years enter and dominate the moving average. Two separate things seem to be happening. During the 1930s, there is a small expansion of non-manual opportunity. Second, there is a 'war effect' which we come to in a moment.

To suggest that there was a growth in the proportions of non-manual work in the 1930s seems on the face of it to ignore the Depression. Even before the start of the decade, the Scottish economy was already depressed chiefly due to its dependence on heavy industry and primary production, sectors hard hit by post-First World War market conditions. Unemployment was running at around 15 per cent during the 1920s and reached a peak in 1932 when one in every four Scots was out of a job: in steel, coal and shipbuilding the figure was more often between 40 and 60 per cent. 'The hard core of unemployment which persisted throughout the interwar period is traceable to the old staple industries, in particular mining, shipbuilding, iron and steel, textiles and mechanical engineering.' It was not until 1942 that unemployment returned to 'normal' levels (Harvie, 1977, pp. 168–74; Slaven, 1975; Kellas, 1968, p. 243; HMSO, 1971, Tables nos. 165–6; Glyn and Oxborrow, 1976, p. 93; Lenman, 1977).

Nevertheless, as Glyn and Oxborrow point out, the interwar years were years of increasing productivity, even in the old staple industries which formed such a significant part of the Scottish economy. There was 'rapid technological progress, and this was not confined to any particular group of industries' (1976, p. 93). Furthermore, the period saw considerable economic concentration as Pollard, Stevenson, Harvie and Hobsbawm have variously shown. Larger units of production require more complex administrative structures, and can support more technical specialists. In other words, there was an expansion of non-manual opportunities even in industries with a poor economic performance.

These brief observations on economic conditions (for more details see Payne, 1986) serve two purposes. First, the transition to increased proportions of non-manual employment can perhaps be partially explained in terms of the occupational requirement of the new technologies and new scales of organisation, which despite high levels of unemployment were maintained throughout the decade. It would seem that young workers benefited from these changes, while their elders tended to remain unemployed, trapped in their increasingly redundant careers. Second, it follows that changes in non-manual employment and upward mobility do not seem to be incompatible with high unemployment, with rising productivity, or with marked changes in the nature of capital.

One 'test' of this interpretation, which will not be reported in any detail here, is to take industries which were declining or expanding during the interwar years, basically as indicated by Leser and Silvey (1950). These do not include all industries (e.g. service industries are omitted) but for the remainder it offers a chance to look for any pattern of association between economic performance (growth or contraction of labour force) and either percentage of non-manual jobs or upward mobility. First, we observe that as far as young men are concerned, there is no evidence that consistently fewer were recruited into the declining industries, even if the total labour force in those industries was falling. Second, while the proportion of non-manual jobs was lower for this group, it grew from around 5 per cent to 10 per cent during the 1930s of which around one-third involved upward mobility. In the expanding industries, non-manual jobs made up about 20 per cent of all jobs for those first starting work, with a slight tendency for this to be higher in the later years. Up to about half of these jobs went to the upwardly mobile. We therefore conclude that while expansion and relative economic success are associated with growth in non-manual occupations and mobility, the same process is going on, to a lesser extent, even in contracting and economically unsuccessful industries. This conclusion applies, however, only to those entering work for the first time: the experience of older men may be much less optimistic.

But if the transition to higher levels of non-manual employment is sufficiently robust to stand up to the effects of the Depression, how is one to explain the collapse of this trend (and mobility rates) in the late forties and 1950s? (See Figure 7.1, years plotted between 1940 and 1950, but remembering which years are included in the moving averages.) We would like tentatively to suggest that this is the result of a quite separate process, namely a 'war effect'.

The war economy differed from that of peacetime in several important ways. First, a very large part of the male labour force was not available for employment, because they were in the armed forces. Calder records that one-sixth of men under 40, and more than half of men in their twenties, had been called up by July 1940 (1971, pp. 138 and 481–2). Second, 'non-essential' enterprises were run down or suspended, while industries directly relevant to the war effort were modified and expanded. Third, the need for coordination, rapid change and controls generated new state bureaucracies and company record-keeping departments.

The processes through which school-leavers were recruited to fill vacant jobs were therefore completely different during this period. The data on which Figure 7.1 is based refer only to civilian jobs or regular armed forces employment: young men volunteering for or conscripted into the armed forces are excluded. The school leaver taking a civilian job between 1939 and 1945 found himself able to consider jobs which under normal circumstances would not have been available to him. Men of fighting age were being replaced by women, by old men past retirement age, and by these youngsters. In a situation of economic upheaval and labour shortage, established practices were in abeyance and the inexperienced could find themselves taken on in offices or stores, or (given the prevalent attitudes of the time) used to direct the labours of women (see Pelling, 1963; Cole and Postgate, 1961).

Thus the rise shown in Figure 7.1 in the numbers of non-manual occupations and in the upward mobility rate do not reflect so much an expansion of the non-manual sector, but in the increased employment of young men in those non-manual occupations that were available. What we are witnessing is a temporary change in recruitment patterns. To put it another way, the graphs show at this point an improvement in the chances of the young worker getting a non-manual job as well as any structural shift caused by the newly created machinery of state regulation.

Conversely, after the war, the reverse was true. Not only were there the demobbed armed forces back in contention, but those who had done so well at home during the war were also well-ensconced in their careers. The opportunities for young men entering the labour market for the first time in the post-war period were blocked by older men who had stronger claims than they did. If this supposition is correct then the peak and trough that lie between 1938 and 1949 (i.e. cohorts 1936–40 to 1947–51) are a direct product of the Second World War, and in that sense a deviation from mainstream trends. Its effect in terms of career entry, and therefore subsequent life chance, persists until the end of the 1940s, when the economy had readjusted to peacetime conditions.

From around the early 1950s, non-manual growth is fairly consistent, as one might expect in two peaceful decades marked by more or less steady economic growth, further technological innovation, the flowering of the welfare state, and ever greater economic concentration. What is interesting about this period is the relative decline in upward mobility which appears from the 1955–9 cohort onwards. Clearly, an argument based on the expansion of the non-manual sector alone could not explain the change in mobility rates. Nor can we provide an explanation in terms of changes in opportunity for school leavers, as we did for the period of the war: obviously there was no commensurate economic dislocation, and the authors know of no evidence to suggest that employers modified their patterns of recruitment in some way which discriminated against people from working-class backgrounds. Indeed, if anything we would expect the reverse, as the 1960s are normally depicted as the decade in which new social mores became established, with greater acceptance of working-class etiquette, dialect and mannerisms. The 'swinging sixties' are the years in which British society is supposed to have become more open, so why is this not reflected in the mobility rate?

SOME COMPONENTS OF MOBILITY

The answer to this problem lies in the ways that expansions in non-manual occupations, and mobility, are generated. Despite the implicit assumption of macro-level analysis, these expansions are not a single, uniform, cohesive movement, but merely the sum of several alternative processes. It may be useful to explain this in terms of a simplified model containing only a single industry. Once the principles have been established, we can generalise to a real world in which there are many industries, comprising at least three major industrial sectors experiencing different economic conditions. Our diagrammatic representation is shown in Figure 7.2.

The first part of Figure 7.2 shows an industry with two levels of job, manual and non-manual. The non-manual jobs are subdivided into two by virtue of their recruitment: one part is filled by workers from non-manual origins and the other is filled from manual origins. The number

Figure 7.2 A model of mobility components

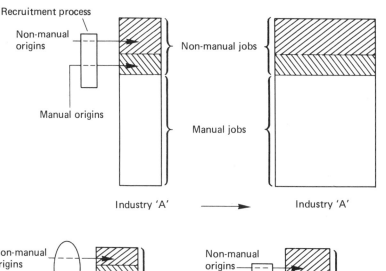

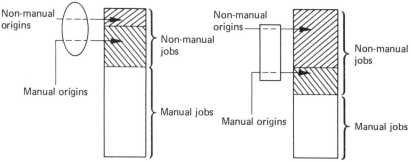

of those coming from manual backgrounds can be expressed as a percentage of all those in the industry, for an industry-specific mobility rate, or more commonly aggregated wth their equivalents in all other industries to give a total mobility rate. On the left of the industry 'block' is a representation of the 'recruitment process'. This is a catchall title to cover everything from the hiring and firing policies of the industry's personnel departments, through the aspirations and values of the total labour force, to the exigencies of the educational system.

In the second part of Figure 7.2 the total size of the same hypothetical industry has increased, as represented by a broadening of its width. The industry-specific mobility rate remains the same, but the industry's contribution to total mobility in the society is greater, because more people are going through the expanded industry's 'mobility route'.

In the third part of Figure 7.2 we have returned the industry to its original scale, but modified the recruitment process. Now more of the available non-manual jobs go to the upwardly mobile. Both the industry-specific and the total mobility rates increase. The change in the recruitment process could be something completely external to the industry and thus 'forced' on the employer, or it could be a conscious change in personnel policy which had the (possibly unintended) consequences of opening up access to the children of manual workers.

Finally, we have an industry of the same size, with the original recruitment process, but with an expanded non-manual sector. If these jobs are filled in the same proportions of recruits from manual and non-manual origins as before, there are nonetheless more opportunities for upward mobility in the expanded sector, so that again both the industry-specific and total mobility rates rise. Although each of these processes is analytically separate, in practice they are all operating, to various extents, at the same time. Nor have we exhausted all logical possibilities in identifying these three sources of change: for example, a drastic change in the distribution of origins (by means of a demographic shift or a change in occupational structure) would alter the supply of labour with particular backgrounds and who could be said to be 'at risk' of being upwardly mobile. However, there is no sign of a shift in father's occupation which would explain the pattern reported in Figure 7.1.

If we wish to put some flesh on the bones of this outline, the periods of the thirties and the fifties are ones which can be seen as best represented by the last case.[1] There appears to have been a general increase, in all industries, of non-manual employment. In addition, we can suggest that the expansion of the new, more technological industries in the 1930s, and the welfare state in the early 1950s, represents good examples of our first process, that is a faster expansion of some industries with high non-manual levels than those industries with lower non-manual requirements. The 1940s – or at least the war part of it – provide a concrete example of changing recruitment patterns, as proposed in the third part of Figure 7.2.

Where then, do the 1960s fit into this scheme? The answer lies in our earlier observation that in a real world of many industries, there are differentials in expansion rates and in recruitment practices between industries. The expansion of non-manual employment in the 1960s was located in different sectors, and was of a different kind than in earlier years. In order to see how this works empirically, we need to examine changes in industrial sectors and how each contributes to the overall occupation structure and gross mobility rate.

DISAGGREGATING OCCUPATIONS AND INDUSTRIAL
SECTORS

In disaggregating mobility, we can begin by observing that the four non-manual occupational classes (see Table 7.1) have different historical profiles. Classes II and III tend to show an increasing contribution to overall mobility in the latter part of the period, class I fluctuates between 15 per cent and 20 per cent, and class IV declines. These 'contributions' are a product both of size of class and recruitment processes. For example, class I combines a small increase in scale (from 4 per cent to 10 per cent of the sample) with a decrease of about 10 per cent in its recruitment from manual origins: the net effect is that its contribution to upward mobility tends to be relatively stable and if anything very slightly less towards the end of the period than earlier. Class II's contribution seems to be mainly dominated by its fluctuations in recruitment, rather than by its expansion, although this generalisation does not hold true for the last five years when the size increases while its recruitment decreases.

Class III is not noticeably larger than the others, but it generates at least one-third of all mobility, and as much as half of the total in the early 1940s. Its profile most closely follows the 'war effect' curve. Class IV is relatively small, but has high mobility rates until the late 1950s, when its size contracts further, its upward recruitment drops sharply, and its contribution to total mobility falls from 29 per cent to 5 per cent over the seven years in which overall mobility is in fact climbing.

Thus we find the classes differ in their profiles, and change over time. While expansion in size and to a lesser extent in upward mobility rates is the more common pattern, this is not universal. Nor is there evidence to show that when a class is expanding, manual workers automatically stand a better chance of recruitment (e.g. class II), whereas when a class contracts (briefly, for classes III and IV) this does seem to disadvantage those from manual origins.

The occupations which make up these classes are found in varying degrees in the main industrial sectors. Thus staple industries (coal, steel, shipbuilding, textiles: Standard Industrial Classification minimal list headings nos. 101–9, 261–3, 311–23, 370 and 411–29; HMSO 1968b) have a distinctively low proportion of managerial and professional grades, with in later years fewer routine white-collar workers and more semi-professional and technical staff. For their size, the staples contribute more to upward mobility than the rest of Scotland's industries, for all four non-manual classes.

We can contrast this with the rest of manufacturing (light industry, Standard Industrial Classification minimal list headings nos. 211–499 excluding staples), which have lower than average proportions of classes I and II, but in which the former increases after 1950 while the latter slightly decreases after 1955. Class III is, perhaps surprisingly, lower than average: in this it resembles the staples. There is no clear pattern of recruitment, but in the post-war period there is some move to increases in both scale and upward mobility. Turning to the 'basic services' of construction, transport and distribution (Standard Industrial Classification minimal list headings nos 500–832), we find low proportions of class II (10 per cent compared with 30 per cent overall, towards the end of the period) and high proportions of class III (45 per cent and 20 per cent). However, this dissimilar occupational mix is recruited in a pattern generally typical of the whole sample.

The remaining sector of 'new services' (Standard Industrial Classification minimal list headings nos 860–906), based on organisation and high knowledge levels in commerce and the state, have more non-manual jobs than the other three. In the 1930s, this was just under 40 per cent of all non-manual jobs; by the 1950s this had grown to 45 per cent, and by the later 1960s it was over 50 per cent. It is only in the later years, however, that it comes to dominate classes I and II. In other words, in terms of the earlier discussion in Chapter 4, the new services (Bell's quaternary and quinary sectors) blossom in the 1950s, whereas Moore and other writers' managerial and technical upgrading of skills across all sectors operates from a much earlier point. But in the former blossoming, the amount of upward mobility is almost without exception *lower* than the sample average. We can attach some values to these patterns by comparing the first and last decades as in Table 7.4. The largest shifts in contribution have been between *basic* and *new services*, with a reversal of their positions. *Light industry* is virtually unchanged, both in terms of mobility and number of jobs. But whereas *basic services* were initially contributing a share of mobility consonant with their size, they are now not much smaller but with a large drop in mobility, while *new services* have nearly doubled both employment and mobility. *Old staples* have dropped sharply on both counts.

The dynamics within each sector are presented in Table 7.5, which can be regarded as giving a concrete example of Figure 7.2. Each sector is shown with its actual ('observed') numbers of non-manual or mobile men compared with a series of expected values derived from a shift-share analysis, in which the 'observed' numbers have been standardised to the 1930s level by weighting up each observation by 725/701 (i.e.

Table 7.4 Sectoral share of upward mobility, 1930–9 and 1960–9

		Old staples	Light industry	Basic services	New services	
1930–9	Mobility	13.8	15.0	43.8	27.5	*n*=80
	Size	24.0	18.5	41.9	15.6	*n*=725
1960–9	Mobility	8.4	16.0	27.7	47.7	*n*=119
	Size	14.8	20.5	38.4	27.5	*n*=701

Table 7.5 Intrasectoral changes, 1930–9 and 1960–9

		Old staples	Light industry	Basic services	New services
No. non-manual:	observed	33	35	73	157
	expected*	11	23	54	106
No. of upmobiles:	observed	10	20	34	59
	expected**	20	21	42	58

*Non-manual 1930s × total 1960s
 total 1930s
**Upmobiles 1930s × total non-manual 1960s
 total non-manuals 1930s

1.034) and rounding to the nearest whole number. If one expected value is close to the observed value, but a second is not, this shows which of the Figure 7.2 factors has changed most.

Perhaps the most straightforward pattern is to be found in the *light industry* column. Here, there are more non-manual jobs for the size of the sector in the 1960s than would be expected on the basis of the 1930s (35 compared with 23). But once we know the actual number of non-manuals, we can accurately predict the number of upwardly mobile men (20 observed against a prediction of 21). We can therefore say, in terms of Figure 7.2, that *light industry* has expanded its base (Table 7.4, 18.5 per cent to 20.5 per cent), has more of its jobs now non-manual (Table 7.5, 35, not 23) but has retained basically the same pattern of recruitment to those modified jobs. Precisely the same logic applies to the *new services*: the internal recruitment rate is unchanged, but the scale of process has been increased so that more individuals experience mobility, and the overall mobility rate is increased. Thus a substantial part of each of the two intakes can be thought of as part of a changing mobility experience governed more by scale changes than by association changes.

The picture for the other two sectors – the two industrial groupings which by contrast are in relative and absolute decline – is that the observed levels of non-manual employment are also higher than expected on the basis of the 1930s rates, but the mobility rates are lower. The increase in the non-manual sectors is associated with a recruitment rules change, making it less likely that upward mobility will take place. In the *old staples*, much of the non-manual growth was in class II, and in the *basic services* it was class III. In each class, the mobility associated with these changes tended to be at, or below, the overall trends, i.e. the added non-manual jobs were precisely in those classes where less mobility was taking place.

The key recruitment rule is probably educational qualification for the job. Allowing for the fact that we continue to use broad categories, the relationship between getting a non-manual job (upward mobility and non-manual immobility) and educational qualification becomes closer in the 1960s, compared with the 1930s.

Table 7.6 Mobility and educational qualifications: % with high qualifications

	Upward mobility		Non-manual immobility	
Industrial sector	1930s	1960s	1930s	1960s
Old staples	50.0	50.0	22.2	56.3
Light manufacturing	41.7	42.9	40.0	71.4
Basic services	16.7	38.7	44.4	47.1
New services	34.8	40.4	69.0	71.9
Whole sample*	13.8	31.7	13.8	31.7

*i.e. those with high qualification (A level General Certificate of Education equivalent or better) in the cohort (excluding primary industry) regardless of mobility.

The most significant change is in the new services, because this is the sector which, as we have seen, comes to dominate the supply of non-manual jobs (157 non-manual jobs are in the new services, out of a total of 298 non-manual jobs for all four sectors; see Table 7.5). In other words, the explanation for the lack of increase in overall upward mobility (Figure 7.1) would seem to owe a great deal to the concentration of new employment in the one sector that requires educational qualifications – qualifications which are known to be more accessible to the children of non-manual workers.

This last point is another of the issues in mobility research that warrants a fuller treatment. However, the purpose of introducing it, like the other elements of this chapter, is not to present an exhaustive empirical picture of mobility. The intention has mainly been to illustrate how mobility begins to look from the occupational perspective. Even in providing such an illustration, it has not been possible to introduce all of the potential features which were identified earlier in the book: this fuller treatment is the subject of another, more empirical book (Payne, 1986) but it is hoped that the reader's imagination has been at least partly captured by this chapter's attempt to relate the book's theoretical perspective to some concrete examples.

8 Mobility in Modern Society

In considering mobility as an occupational process, we have drawn heavily on a selection of themes from the two main theories of contemporary society. From the Marxist tradition, the key element is the need of advanced capitalism to develop and organise its elaborate commercial transactions and its state apparatus. While it can be argued that Marxist accounts of the scale of the new occupations thus created, and their role in the class struggle, are less than satisfactory, we do at least have the germ of an understanding of occupational transition. Furthermore, we also have reasons for its occurrence, which are historical and based in the human motives of power and profit that are so evident in our experience of the everyday world. Despite the confusion of the internal disputes between post-Marxists, the political future of these new occupational groups is crucial in explaining current and future social developments.

It is precisely this historical, human and political edge that is lacking in so much of the theoretical work on post-industrial society. What the latter offers instead is a more advanced description of occupational and industrial change, with technological innovation singled out as the key mechanism. In dealing with the detail of change, the notion of two opposing classes disappears, but it is not replaced by alternative credible models of either political processes or human action. The *deus ex machina* is a machine.

In trying to operate between these two schools, the core position of this book has been that we need to know more about occupational groups before attempting to allocate them a class identity or historical role. If we find that they do not fit neatly into our schemes, then it is the schemes which must change, not the reality of the complex occupational patterns. Sadly for sociological theory, human behaviour does tend to be bewilderingly complicated once time is taken to study it.

The purpose of this account is to make the case for looking at mobility in a new way. The task of actually doing mobility analysis on such a basis, and the results that would flow from it, lies beyond the scope of this book, although in the previous chapter some illustrations were offered. It is a considerable way forward to see that industrial sectors

146

have very different occupational processes in terms of mobility opportunities. It is even more important to begin to see how these change the chances of mobility for successive generations. Given that other Scottish Mobility Study data (not reported here) show little variation in subsequent careers, the trend analysis of first job mobility is a challenge both to conventional sociological wisdom and to politicians who argue that Britain is an open (or totally closed) society.

Britain is not an open society. Family background still has a major influence on occupational destinations. The opportunities for working-class children to obtain middle-class jobs, with all the material and social advantages they entail, have *not* improved in recent years. The moral outrage that informed so much of British writing on the inequalities of class and mobility is justified.

But that moral outrage (or ideological commitment) must not blind the social scientist to the high rates of occupational fluidity that typify modern society. Most people experience, through the generations of their own families, a degree of upward mobility. This must be the starting point for any more complex theorising about class formation and identity. Indeed, a new approach needs to go beyond the framework imposed by the mobility studies of the 1970s. What we have so far is an account of male mobility measures by four employment points. It defines out unemployment, not least the unemployment and quasi-employment of young school-leavers who may go for years without having a proper job. It defines out female experiences of employment: the Oxford study omits females, while the Scottish study collected data on the wives of the male respondents which have had to be analysed separately (see Payne *et al.*, 1983a). It defines out economic activity which does not fit neatly under a single occupational title: moon-lighting, self-provisioning, even the complexity of occupational tasks themselves cannot be easily accommodated. It defines out the special experiences of disadvantaged minority groups; blacks, the physically disabled, or 'deviants'.

Of course, it is not mobility analysis *per se* that suffers from these limitations. Any problem of the occupation/class interface applies to mobility studies, because they deal in movements between occupations and classes. Until a new theoretical paradigm can be established for the 1980s, mobility will be trapped in a partial account of overall processes. That should not be seen as a total condemnation of the endeavour: there should be less disgrace in doing only part of the work, and more recognition of how large that work as a whole is likely to be.

The danger with pointing out some of the limits of mobility analysis is that we then write off *everything* that such work can offer. It has already been observed above that a lot of empirical evidence is still to come. We do not, for instance, have any details of *intra*generational mobility, the patterns of how individuals' careers are structured after their first jobs. The idea of labour markets and mobility has only been raised, but not documented.There has only been one brief reference to education, and the analysis of sectoral differences has been cursory. None of this has been fitted into an actual historical account of occupational change in a given society. In other words, there is still a lot of interesting mobility information to come, which even in its limited way, will change the understanding of occupational processes (Payne, 1986).

But what is more important is the recognition that *mobility matters*. Mobility, despite its dressing up in operational definitions and statistical technicalities, is a phenomenon of everyday experience. At a simple level, 'getting on in life' and 'getting a job' are concerns of parents for their children, or a common topic of informal conversations among acquaintances. It is part of the common sense world. It is also, at a more complex level, a political issue. Equality of life chances lurks around the ideological statements and party platforms of professional politicians, because mobility *is* so much part and parcel of contemporary society. Social order, so much uncontested for so long in Britain, depends on economic and social conditions among which are numbered chances of getting on, and gross inequalities of condition. The safety valve view of mobility normally stresses how it works: in a world of curtailed mobility the valve may stick.

On the other hand, a more sanguine and less apocalyptical view still calls for the recognition of occupational mobility as a significant factor in social planning. To take a single example, planning higher education requires some forward estimate of demand for student places. Given that we know the propensity to become a student is related to occupation of father, such projections depend on an estimate of both occupational transition and rates of social mobility, so that the relative size of occupational groupings can be forecast (see HMSO, 1984). Present occupation is a useful analytical tool: previous occupations or family background, not least taking account of women's characteristics, will improve sociographic accounting. Demand for higher education has its parallels in housing, medicine and leisure planning, as well as in the commercial field.

Given such an importance, it is not enough simply to describe rates of movements or to discuss them purely in terms of class structures. It is necessary to free discussion of mobility from its prison of stratification.

Once that is done, by recognising the occupational dimension, then a wider repertoire of sociological theories can be brought to bear, in order to *explain* why mobility happens. In turn, the new understanding of occupational mobility can then be fed back into debates about the class structure and how that has evolved this century in the specific historical conditions of advanced capitalism experienced in our society.

Notes

1 Perspectives on Mobility

1. With such a productive and international field as social mobility a comprehensive review would not rise above an annotated bibliography, and indeed the period to 1960 is largely covered by Miller (1960) and Mack *et al.* (1957). Bibby (1975) and Kaelble (1981) also contain surveys. Instead, a number of the more influential studies are discussed with the intention of identifying certain common themes, and, through critique, of justifying why the present account has developed in its particular fashion.
2. See Blau and Duncan, 1967, pp. 163–77. Simple explanations of the technique can also be found in Silvey 1975, p. 113 and more technical accounts can be found in Blalock, 1972. The work of Sewell and others at the Madison Centre for Demography and Ecology at the University of Wisconsin, for example, is typical of the complex elaboration that has been undertaken to model the US status achievement process.
3. To be fair, Lipset and Bendix do make some allowance for the farm/non-farm distinction, but this is still a very crude measure compared with the greater specificity of the original 15 studies (Lipset and Bendix, 1964, p. 13, 4ff.).

2 Mobility, Occupations and Class

1. When the present author outlined this 'sociographic' approach at the SSRC International Mobility Seminar in 1975, it clearly surprised the other participants. Goldthorpe's contribution to that seminar (later to be published as Goldthorpe and Llewellyn, 1977) was subsequently revised to take in a new section on changes in the occupational structure, exactly as proposed (Payne *et al.*, 1975). However, this remains the only (and a very partial) British attempt to connect mobility to its historical context.
2. It should be noted however that Goldthorpe regards himself as working precisely within Lockwood's framework: see Goldthorpe (1982, pp. 169–70); Hope and Goldthorpe (1974) on the original construction of the scale; and note 8 in the *draft* of Goldthorpe and Llewellyn (1977) (in the published version this is reduced to a simple reference to *The Blackcoated Worker*).

3 Occupations in Capitalist Society

1. Although this account has been presented in ideal typical terms, in order to point up the particular character of labour under capitalism, it also reflects the heavy historical emphasis of this school of social analysis.
2. For example, Marx and Engels (1962, p. 41); Marx (1969, p. 300); Marx (1959a, p. 293), although passing references to multiple classes or strata are numerous in his work (see Evans, 1975, pp. 80–1). Obviously, there is a

danger of oversimplification if one concentrates too narrowly on the 'two class' aspect of Marx's work. However, an emphasis on domination and the two major classes is not incompatible with recognising the importance of the minor classes (see, for example, Wesolowski, 1979, Part 1). Harris's discussion (1939, 328–32) of the middle class in Marx shows how oversimplification can be avoided by appeal to the overall balance of Marx's writings. The polemicist of the *Manifesto* is not to be taken as representing the scientist of the *18th Brumaire* or *Capital* (Harris, 1959, pp. 333–4).
3. The slightly repetitive list is drawn from various sources in Marx's writing; see Harris (1939, pp. 349, 352–3) for original references.

4   Occupations in Post-Industrial Society

1. Many of these accounts are lacking in historical accuracy, operate with imprecise occupational categories, deal inconsistently with rates of change, fail to account for deviant case, and lack specification of causal relationships. For a fuller discussion, see Payne, 1977a and 1977b.

5   Class and Labour Markets in Contemporary Society

1. Although it is interesting to note that Giddens seems to think in terms of 'class mobility', not occupational or social mobility: see the index entries (or rather, absence of them) for these terms, 1973; pp. 327, 332 and 334.
2. With which, it may be pointed out, many white male trade unionists would sympathise. Obviously, in dealing with such 'non-economic' or 'non-technological' criteria, we are moving some way beyond the theory of industrial society. Writers such as Blackburn could equally well be treated as part of the Marxist tradition, although his inclusion here enables the question of market segmentation to be more easily linked to the labour needs of certain technologies.

6   *Social Mobility in Britain*: The Old Evidence

1. Parts of this chapter discusses in very considerable detail those parts of *Social Mobility in Britain* dealing explicitly with intergenerational social mobility: the reader may find it helpful to have a copy to hand. Criticisms of *Social Mobility in Britain* made below refer not to all parts of that book, but to the specific sections on this type of mobility, Glass, e.g. 1954, pp. 179–215. The reader who is less interested in empirical evidence or is totally innumerate may choose to skip this chapter.
2. The pattern of fertility since 1880 is as shown in the following table:

Differential fertility

	Live births for completed families		
Date	(a) Non-manual*	(b) Manual	Ratio (b) to (a)
1880–1886	4.35	5.87	1.35
1887–1889	—	—	—
1890–1899	3.50	4.83	1.38
1900–1909	2.81	3.96	1.41
1910–1914	2.36	3.36	1.42
1915–1919	2.07	2.94	1.42
1920–1924	1.90	2.72	1.43

*Glass and Grebennick use a variety of classifications, most notably 'manual' and 'non-manual'; and 'status group I' and 'status group II', which seem to be the same. The three sources in the table all use the manual/non-manual classification. It should be remembered that the absolute levels of fertility are subject to effects such as differential age at marriage, and mortality. However, the authors argue that the ratio does not change very much if corrections are made: For example Table 35, p. 106, gives Status I : Status II ratios for the 1900s as 1.41; 1.41; 1.40 and 1.41.
SOURCES: Glass and Grebennick, 1954: 1880–6: Table in footnote 2, p. 108, 1890–9: Table 36, p. 107, remainder: Table 5, p. 4.

An alternative method of calculation is to take the number of men reporting fathers in each category, divide by the fertility rate, and then weight up the results by the necessary factor to reproduce the original total number of fathers. This can be done for each decade, drawing from Glass's (1954) tables 1 and 6, and 6.2, e.g. for pre-1898 births:

1	Listed non-manual fathers	250	Listed manual fathers		429
2	Divided by non-manual fertility	2.13	Divided by manual fertility		2.94
3	Gives	117	Gives		145.9
4	Which weighted up by		Which weighted up by		
	2.582 i.e. $\dfrac{679}{(117+146)}$ =	302	2.582 i.e. $\dfrac{679}{(117+146)}$ =		377

This system applied to each decade provides a weighted estimate of 39.7 per cent non-manual and 60.3 per cent manual, as against the more straightforward estimate of 40.4 per cent and 59.6 per cent, i.e. using Glass's categories 5, 6 and 7 because Miller does not provide sufficient detail to repeat our earlier calculations. The difference between the reported and 'real' figures is around 7 percentage points using Glass's data, or 8.1 per cent using the alternative method.

3. As Table 6.1 (page 95) showed, the male workforce for England and Wales was 11,744,994 in 1921. Had the non-manual class made up the same proportion of that total as in 1951 – 35.1 per cent – then there would have been 4,122,493 non-manuals, an expansion of 602,789 on 3,519,704 (the number of non-manuals in 1921). That is, an expansion due to occupational transition, but controlling for the growth of the labour market, of 17.1 per cent.

   The contraction of 18 per cent is given by taking the difference between the son's distribution as reported by Miller (1295 non-manual) and the estimated 'real' father's distribution (i.e. allowing for differential fertility) of 45.2 per cent of 3497, that is 1582 non-manual. The difference of 287 is expressed as a percentage of 1582 (18.1 per cent).

4. The concentration of overrepresentation in categories 4 and 5a is important, because they have particular mobility characteristics which ramify throughout the mobility matrix. In general, lower grade supervisory staff (e.g. foremen) and routine grades of non-manual work (e.g. clerks and shop assistants) are among those categories more likely to be recruited from a wide range of backgrounds (Goldthorpe, 1975, p. 9–10). In the Scottish Mobility Study, the coding of supervisors and inspectors proved technically difficult and despite detailed checks and recodings, the eventual sample showed about 8 per cent foremen, compared with the 1971 Census figure of 5 per cent (although these figures are not for strictly compatible populations and the census figure *should* be marginally lower). Presumably this is a self-inflation effect, and it may be that part of the problem with the Glass data arises from a similar phenomenon.

   Among other very helpful comments on an earlier draft of this chapter Trevor Noble has pointed out the difficulty of allocating SEG 8 (service workers) who should really be split between Hall–Jones categories Va and VI. If SEG 8 is reclassified as manual as Noble has done, then the Glass/census comparison becomes 37/31.3 per cent, which is more in line with his criticism of the sample.

5. There is one speculation arising from personal correspondence and informal conversations which might fit the bill, but it must be stressed that *it is highly speculative*. In the Glass questionnaire, it is said that the father's and son's main jobs were on the same page. If the father's job was insufficiently detailed, it is possible that the easy availability of the more detailed son's job might have influenced the coding decision on the father. A coder unconsciously believing that there was little social mobility might have been guided to allocate the father into the same category as the son. For example, if a father was an 'engineer', and the son a factory manager, the father might be located as a professional engineer rather than a skilled manual worker (as the discussion of mobility in the industrial sector, p. 41, shows, this could be no small factor). The net effect would be to make fathers occupationally like their sons, increasing the former's proportions of non-manual posts, reducing apparent mobility and increasing self-recruitment – which fits neatly with the objections raised so far in this chapter, except for Ridge's finding that the brothers have been 'downgraded'. As the brothers' jobs were recorded on a separate page of the questionnaire, *perhaps* there was less contamination, although this seems a weak explanation.

7　The New Account of Mobility

1. The reader should not be misled by the convenience of terms like 'the 1950s' or the '1960s' into thinking about these decades as neat periods. Using rolling cohorts enables us to be flexible in our analysis, and to see when a trend begins or finishes, but this still involves some interminency at either end of a period containing a trend, and the definition of a period is based on its mobility and occupational characteristics. If, in addition, the mobility profile changes at a time when the economy undergoes a shift (as evidenced by other sources) this reinforces the argument that economy and mobility are linked, rather than being taken as evidence for an aggressively periodic view of recent history.

Bibliography

Aaronovitch, S. (1955) *Monopoly: A Study of British Monopoly Capitalism* (Lawrence and Wishart, London).

Abercrombie, N. and Urry, J. (1982) *Capital, Labour and the Middle Classes* (Allen and Unwin, London).

Adams, B. N. (1968) *Kinship in an Urban Setting* (Markham, Chicago).

Allen, B. and Bytheway, W. (1973) 'The Effects of Differential Fertility on Sampling in Studies of Intergenerational Social Mobility', *Sociology*, vol. 7, no. 2.

Anderson, P. (1974) *Passages from Antiquity to Feudalism* (New Left Books, London).

Appelbaum, R. (1971) *Theories of Social Change* (Markham, Chicago).

Aron, R. (1967a) *The Industrial Society* (Praeger, New York).

Aron, R. (1967b) *18 Lectures on Industrial Society* (Weidenfeld and Nicolson, London).

Averitt, R. T. (1965) *The Dual Economy: The Dynamics of American Industry Structure* (Free Press, Glencoe).

Bain, G. *et al.* (1972) 'The Labour Force', in A. H. Halsey (ed.) *Trends in British Society since 1900* (Macmillan, London).

Banks, J. A. (1954) *Prosperity and Parenthood* (Routledge and Kegan Paul, London).

Banks, J. A. (1964) 'The Structure of Industrial Enterprise in Industrial Society', in P. Halmos (ed.) *The Development of Industrial Societies*. Sociological Review Monograph No. 8, University of Keele.

Banks, J. A. (1967) 'The BSA – The First 15 Years', *Sociology*, vol. 1, no. 1.

Baran, P. (1957) *The Political Economy of Growth* (Calder, London).

Barron, R. and Norris, G. (1976) 'Sexual Divisions and the Dual Labour Market', in D. Barker and S. Allen (eds) *Dependence and Exploitation in Work and Marriage* (Longmans, London).

Bechhofer, F. (1969) 'Occupation', in M. Stacey (ed.) *Comparability in Social Research* (Heinemann, London).

Bell, C. (1968) *Middle Class Families* (Routledge and Kegan Paul, London).

Bell, D. (1974) *The Coming of Post Industrial Society* (Heinemann, London).

Bendix, R. and Lipset, S. M. (1959) *Social Mobility and Industrial Society* (University of California Press, Los Angeles).

Benjamin, B. (1958) 'Inter-Generational Differences in Occupation', *Population Studies*, vol. XI.

Berle, A. and Means, G. (1932) *The Modern Corporation and Private Property* (Macmillan, New York).

Bertaux, D. (1969) 'Sur l'analyse des tables de mobilité sociale', *Revue Française de Sociologie*, vol. X.

Bibby, J. (1975) 'Methods of Measuring Mobility', *Quality and Quantity*, vol. 9, no. 2.

Blackburn, R. and Mann, M. (1979) *The Working Class in the Labour Market* (Macmillan, London).

Blalock, H. (1972) *Social Statistics* (McGraw-Hill, London).

Blau, P. and Duncan, O. (1967) *The American Occupational Structure* (Wiley, New York).

Bottomore, T. (1965) *Classes in Modern Society* (Allen and Unwin, London).

Braverman, H. (1974) *Labour and Monopoly Capitalism* (Monthly Press Review, New York).

Browning, H. L. and Singlemann, J. (1978) 'The Transformation of the US Labour Force', in *Politics and Society*, vol. 8, no. 4.

Burnham, J. (1945) *The Managerial Revolution* (Penguin, Harmondsworth).

Busfield, J. and Paddon, M. (1977) *Thinking about Children* (Cambridge University Press, Cambridge).

Butler, D. and Stokes, D. (1969) *Political Change in Britain* (Macmillan, London).

Calder, A. (1971) *The People's War* (Panther, London).

Caradog Jones, D. (ed.) (1934) *The Social Survey of Merseyside*, vol. 2, (University Press of Liverpool, London).

Carchedi, G. (1975) 'On the Economic Identification of the New Middle Class', *Economy and Society*, vol. 4, no. 1.

Carchedi, G. (1977) *On the Economic Identification of Social Classes* (Routledge and Kegan Paul, London).

Carr-Saunders, A. M., Caradog Jones, D. and Moser, C. (1958) *A Survey of Social Conditions in England and Wales as Illustrated by Statistics* (Oxford University Press, Oxford).

Chessa, F. (1912) *La Trasmissione Ereditaria della Professioni* (Fratelli Bocca, Editori, Turin).

Chinoy, E. (1955) 'Social Mobility Trends in the United States', *American Sociological Review* vol. 20, no. 2.

Clapham (1946) *Report of the Committee on the Provision for Social and Economic Research* (HMSO, London).

Clarke, E. (1957) *The Conditions of Economic Progress* (3rd edn) (Macmillan, London).

Clegg, S. and Dunkerley, D. (1980) *Organization, Class and Control* (Routledge and Kegan Paul, London).

Cole, G. D. H. and Postgate, R. (1961) *The Common People* (Methuen, London).

Cotgrove, S. (1967) *The Science of Society* (2nd edn) (Allen and Unwin, London).

Crompton, R. (1980) 'Class Mobility and Modern Britain', *Sociology*, vol. 14, no. 1.

Crompton, R. and Gubbay, J. (1977) *Economy and Class Structure* (Macmillan, London).

Crosland, A. (1956) *The Future of Socialism* (Cape, London).

Crowder, N. D. (1974) 'A Critique of Duncan's Stratification Research', *Sociology*, vol. 8, no. 1.

Cutright, P. (1968) 'Occupational Inheritance', *American Journal of Sociology*, vol. 73, no. 1.

Dahrendorf, R. (1959) *Class and Class Conflict in Industrial Society* (Routledge and Kegan Paul, London).

Dahrendorf, R. (1982) *On Britain* (BBC Publications, London).

Davies, M. (1979) *Beyond Class Images* (Croom Helm, London).

Doeringer, D. G. and Piore, M. J. (1971) *International Labour Markets and Manpower Analysis* (D. C. Heath, New York).

Duncan-Jones, P. (1972) 'Social Mobility, Economical Scoring and Occupational Classification', in K. Hope (ed.) (1972) *The Analysis of Social Mobility* (Oxford University Press, Oxford).

Dunkerley, D. (1979) 'Upgrading or Deskilling?', Unpublished Mss, Plymouth Polytechnic, Plymouth.

Edwards, R. (1980) *Contested Terrain: The Transformation of the Work Place in the Twentieth Century* (Heinemann, London).

Edwards, R. C., Reich, M. and Gordon, D. M. (eds) (1975) *Labour Market Segmentation* (D. C. Heath, Lexington).

Ehrenreich, B. and Ehrenreich, J. (1979) 'The Professional-Managerial Class', in P. Walker (ed.) *Between Labour and Class* (Monthly Review Press, New York).

Erikson, R., Goldthorpe, J. and Portocarero, L. (1979) 'Intergenerational Class Mobility in Three Western European Societies', *British Journal of Sociology* vol. XXX, no. 4.

Erikson, R., Goldthorpe, J. and Portocarero, L. (1981) *Social Fluidity in Industrial Nations: England, France and Sweden*, Swedish Institute for Social Research, Stockholm.

Evans, M. (1975) *Karl Marx* (Allen and Unwin, London).

Feldman, A. and Moore, W. E. (1963) 'Industrialization and Industrialism', *Transactions of the Fifth World Congress of Sociology*, Sep. Washington.

Floud, J. and Halsey, A. (1958) 'The Sociology of Education', *Current Sociology*, vol. 7, no. 3.

Floud, J. and Halsey, A. (1961) 'Introduction', in A. H. Halsey, J. Floud and L. A. Anderson, *Education, Economy and Society* (Collier-Macmillan, London).

Fox, T. and Miller, S. (1965) 'Economic, Political and Social Determinants of Mobility', *Acta Sociologica*, vol. 9, no. 1.

Frankel, M. (1969) *Capitalist Society and Modern Sociology* (Lawrence and Wishart, London).

Fröbel, F., Heinrichs, J. and Kreye, D. (1980) *The New International Division of Labour* (Cambridge University Press, Cambridge).

Galbraith, J. K. (1967) *The New Industrial State* (Hamish Hamilton, London).

Gallie, D. (1978) *In Search of the New Working Class* (Cambridge University Press, London).

Garnsey, E. (1975) 'Occupational Structure in Industrial Societies', *Sociology*, vol. 3, no. 3.

Gershuny, J. (1978) *After Industrial Society?* (Macmillan, London).

Gershuny, J. (1983) *Social Innovation and the Division of Labour* (Oxford University Press, London).

Gershuny, J. and Miles, I. (1983) *The New Service Economy* (Frances Pinter, London).

Giddens, A. (1973) *The Class Structures of the Advanced Societies* (Hutchinson, London).

Giddens, A. and Mackenzie, G. (eds) (1982) *Social Class and the Division of Labour* (Cambridge University Press, London).

Ginsberg, M. (1929) 'Interchange between Social Classes', *Economic Journal*, vol. XXXIX, Dec.

Girod, R. (1974) 'Inégalités des Chances', 8th Congrès Mondial de Sociologie, Toronto, Aug. 1974.

Glass, D. V. (ed.) (1954) *Social Mobility in Britain* (Routledge and Kegan Paul, London).

Glass, D. V. (1969) 'Fertility Trends in Europe since the Second World War', in S. Behrman, L. Corsa, and R. Freedman, (eds) (1969). *Fertility and Family Planning* (University of Michigan Press, Ann Arbor).

Glass, D. V. and Grebennick, D. (1954) *The Trend and Pattern of Fertility in Britain*. Papers of the Royal Commission on Population, vol. 6, (HMSO, London).

Glynn, S. and Oxborrow, J. (1976) *Interwar Britain* (Allen and Unwin, London).

Goldthorpe, J. (1974) *An Introduction to Sociology* (2nd edn) (Cambridge University Press, Cambridge).

Goldthorpe, J. E. (1975) 'Occupational Mobility and Class Structure'. Paper read at the SSRC International Seminar on Social Mobility, Aberdeen, Sep. 1975 (xerox).

Goldthorpe, J. (1980a) *Social Mobility and Class Structure in Modern Britain* (Oxford University Press, Oxford) (with C. Llewellyn and C. Payne).

Goldthorpe, J. (1980b) 'Reply to Crompton', *Sociology*, vol. 14, no. 1, Feb.

Goldthorpe, J. (1982) 'On the Service Class', in A. Giddens, and G. Mackenzie (eds) *Social Class and the Division of Labour* (Cambridge University Press, London).

Goldthorpe, J. and Llewellyn, C. (1977) 'Class Mobility in Modern Britain', *Sociology*, vol. 11, no. 3.

Hakim, C. (1979) *Occupational Segregation*. Dept. of Employment Research Paper no. 9 (Department of Education, London).

Halmos, P. (ed.) (1964) *The Development of Industrial Societies*. Sociological Review Monograph no. 8 (University of Keele, Keele).

Halsey, A. H. (ed.) (1972) *Trends in British Society Since 1900* (Macmillan, London).

Halsey, A. H. (1982) 'Provincials & Professionals', *Archives Européenes de Sociologie*, vol. 23, no. 1.

Halsey, A. H., Heath, A. and Ridge, J. (1980) *Origins and Destinations* (Oxford University Press, Oxford).

Harris, A. L. (1939) 'Pure Capitalism and the Disappearance of the Middle Class', *Journal of Political Economy*, vol. XVIII.

Harris, A. and Clausen, R. (1966) *Labour Mobility in Great Britain, 1953–63*. Government Social Survey (HMSO, London).

Harvie, C. (1977) *Scotland and Nationalism* (Allen and Unwin, London).

Hauser, R. (1978) 'A Structural Model of the Mobility Table', *Social Forces*, vol. 56, no. 3.

Hauser, R., Koffel, J., Travis, H. and Dickinson, P. (1975a) 'Temporal Change in Occupational Mobility', *American Sociological Review*, vol. 40, June.

Hauser, R., Koffel, J., Travis, H. and Dickinson, P. (1975b) 'Structural Change in Occupational Mobility Among Men in the US', *American Sociological Review*, vol. 40, Oct.

Hawthorn, G. (1970) *The Sociology of Fertility* (Collier-Macmillan, London).

Heath, A. (1981) *Social Mobility* (Fontana, London).

Heyworth (1965) *Report of the Committee on Social Studies* (HMSO, London).

Hill, C. (1969) *The Century of Revolution: 1603–1713* (Sphere, London).

Hindess, B. (1981) 'The Politics of Social Mobility', *Economy and Society*, vol. 10, no. 2.

HMSO, (1921, 31, 51, 61) *Census of Scotland, Occupations and Industries Report*, Edinburgh.

HMSO (1968a) *Census 1961, Great Britain. General Report* (HMSO, London, 1968).

HMSO (1968b) *Standard Industrial Classification* (HMSO, London).

HMSO (1971) *British Labour Statistics Historical Abstract 1886–1968* (Department of Employment, London).

HMSO (1971) *Census GB, Economic Activity Tables Pt. IV* (HMSO, London).

HMSO (1984) *The Demand for Higher Education* (DES, ROE 100, London).

Hodges, D. C. (1961) 'The "Intermediate Classes" in Marxist Theory', *Social Research*, vol. 28, no. 3.

Hollingshead, A. B. (1952) 'Trends in Social Stratification', *American Sociological Review*, vol. 17.

Holt, R. T. and Turner, J. E. (eds) (1970) *The Methodology of Comparative Research* (Free Press, Glencoe).

Hope, K. (1975) 'Trends in the Openness of British Society in the Present Century'. Paper circulated at the SSRC International Seminar on Social Mobility, Aberdeen, Sep.

Hope, K. (1980) *Vertical or Class Mobility?* Unpublished ms. (Nuffield College, Oxford).

Hope, K. and Goldthorpe, J. (1974) *The Social Grading of Occupations* (Oxford University Press, Oxford).

Hoselitz, B. (1954) 'Social Stratification and Economic Development', *International Social Science Journal*, vol. 16, no. 2.

Hunt, A. (ed.) (1977) *Class and Class Structure* (Lawrence and Wishart, London).

Jain, H. and Sloane, P. (1977) 'The Disadvantaged in the Labour Market in the Context of North America and Selected European Countries', Research and Working Paper Series, no. 128. Hamilton, Ontario. McMaster University, Faculty of Business, March.

Johnson, T. (1977) 'What Is To Be Kown?' *Economy and Society*, vol. 6, no. 2.

Johnson, T. and Rattansi, A. (1981) 'Social Mobility Without Class', *Economy and Society*, vol. 10, no. 2.

Jones, B. (1982) 'Destruction or Redistribution of Engineering Skills?' in S. Wood (ed.) *The Degradation of Work?* (Hutchinson, London).

Jones, T. (1977) 'Occupational Transition in Advanced Industrial Societies – A Reply', *Sociological Review*, vol. 25, no. 2.

Kaelble, H. (1981) *Historical Research on Social Mobility* (trans Noakes, F.) (Croom Helm, London).

Katouzian, M. A. (1970) 'The Development of the Service Sectors', *Oxford Economic Papers*, no. 22, Nov.

Kaufman, R. L., Smith, C. and Dickson, M. (1981) 'Defrocking Dualism', *Social Science Research*, vol. 10, no. 1.

Kay, G. (1979) *The Economic Theory of the Working Class* (Macmillan, London).

Kellas, J. (1968) *Modern Scotland* (Pall Mall, London).

Kendrick, S., McCrone, D. and Bechhofer, F. (1982) *Industrial and*

Occupational Structure, Working Paper no. 2, Social Structure of Modern Scotland Project, University of Edinburgh.

Kerr, C., Dunlop, J., Harbison, F. and Myers, C. A. (1973) *Industrialism and Industrial Man* (2nd edn) (Penguin, Harmondsworth).

King, R. and Raynor, J. (1981) *The Middle Class* (Longmans, London).

Kolabinska, M. (1912) *La circulation des élites en France*, Lausanne (referred to in Sorokin (1927) *Social Mobility* (Harper, New York).

Kreckel, R. (1973) 'Towards a Theoretical R eorientation of the Sociological Analysis of Vertical Mobility', in W. Müller and K. Mayer (eds) *Social Stratification and Career Mobility* (The Hague, Mouton).

Kreckel, R. (1980) 'Unequal Opportunity Structure and Labour Market Segmentation', *Sociology*, vol. 14, no. 4.

Kumar, K. (1974) 'The Industrializing and the "Post Industrial" Worlds', in T. de Kadt and G. Williams (eds), *Sociology and Development* (Tavistock, London).

Kumar, K. (1976) 'Industrialism and Post-industrialism: Reflections on a Putative Transition', *Sociological Review*, vol. 24, no. 3.

Kuusinen, O. V. *et al.* (1959) *Fundamentals of Marxism-Leninism* (New York, Crowell-Collier and Macmillan).

Kuznets, S. (1957) 'Quantitative Aspects of the Economic Growth of Nations', *Economic Development and Cultural Change*, vol. 5, no. 4.

Lenman, B. (1977) *An Economic History of Modern Scotland* (Batsford, London).

Lenski, G. E. (1958) 'Trends in Intergenerational Occupational Mobility in the United States', *American Sociological Review*, vol. 23, no. 5.

Lenski, G. E. (1970) *Human Societies* (McGraw-Hill, New York).

Leser, C. E. V. and Silvey, H. (1950) 'Scottish Industries during the Inter-War Period', *The Manchester School of Economic and Social Studies*, vol. XVIII, May.

Lipset, S. M. (1960) *Political Man* (Heinemann, London).

Lipset, S. M. and Bendix, R. (1959–64) *Social Mobility in Industrial Society* (Berkeley, University of California Press).

Little, A. and Westergaard, J. (1964) 'The Trends of Class Differentials in Education Opportunity in England and Wales', *British Journal of Sociology*, vol. 15, no. 3.

Litwak, E. (1960a) 'Occupational Mobility and Extended Family Cohesion', *American Sociological Review*, vol. 25, no. 1.

Litwak, E. (1960b) 'Geographical Mobility and Extended Family Cohesion', *American Sociolgical Review*, vol. 25, no. 2.

Lockwood, D. (1958) *The Black Coated Worker* (Allen and Unwin, London).

Loveridge, R. and Mok, A. (1979) *Theories of Labour Market Segmentation* (Martinus Nijhoff, The Hague).

Macdonald, K. (1974) 'The Hall–Jones Scale', in Ridge (1974a) *Mobility in Britain Reconsidered* (Oxford University Press, London).

Mack, R. W., Freeman, S. and Yellin, S. (1957) *Social Mobility: Thirty Years of Research and Theory*. (Syracuse University Press, Syracuse).

Mackay, D. I., Boddy, D., Brack, J., Diack, J. and Jones, N. (1971) *Labour Markets Under Different Employment Conditions* (Allen and Unwin, London).

Mackenzie, G. (1976) 'Class and Class Consciousness' *Marxism Today*, March.

Mackenzie, G. (1982) 'Class Boundaries and the Labour Process', in A. Giddens and G. Mackenzie (eds) *Social Class and the Division of Labour* (Cambridge University Press, Cambridge).

McLellan, D. (1973) *Marx's Grundrisse* (Paladin, London).

Mann, M. (1973) *Workers on the Move* (Cambridge University Press, London).

Marglin, S. (1976) 'What do Bosses Do? – The origins and functions of hierarchy in capitalist production', in A. Gorz (ed.), *The Division of Labour* (Harvester, Sussex).

Marsh, D. (1965) *The Changing Social Structure of England and Wales 1871–1961* (2nd edn) (Routledge and Kegan Paul, London).

Martin, R. and Fryer, R. H. (1973) *Redundancy and Paternalistic Capitalism* (Allen and Unwin, London).

Marx, K. (1969) *Theories of Surplus Value* (Lawrence and Wishart, London).

Marx, K. (1959a) *Capital*, vol. I (Foreign Languages Publishing House, Moscow).

Marx, K. (1959b) *Capital*, vol. III (Lawrence and Wishart, London).

Marx, K. and Engels, F. (1962) *Selected Works*, vol. I (Lawrence and Wishart, London).

Miliband, R. (1969) *The State in Capitalist Society* (Weidenfeld and Nicolson, London).

Miller, S. M. (1960) 'Comparative Social Mobility', *Current Sociology*, vol. 9, no. 1.

Mills, C. W. (1963) 'A Marx for the Managers', in I. L. Horowitz (ed.) *Power, Politics and People* (Oxford University Press, London).

Ministry of Health (1956) *Matters of Life and Death*. Pt. ii (1955) (GRO, London).

Mok, A. (1975) 'Is There a Dual Labour Market in the Netherlands?' (1975) (Is er een dubbele arbeidsmarkt in Nederland?) reproduced in translation from the Dutch as part of R. Loveridge and A. Mok *Theories of Labour Market* (Martinus Nijhoff, The Hague) pp. 123–9.

Monk, D. (1970) *Social Grading on the National Readership Survey*, Joint Industry Committee for National Readership Surveys, London.

Moore, R. (1977) 'Migrants and the Class Structure of Western Europe', in R. Scase (ed.) *Industrial Society: Class, Cleavage and Control* (Allen and Unwin, London).

Moore, W. E. (1963) *Social Change* (Prentice Hall, Englewood Cliffs). 2nd edn 1974.

Müller, W. (1977) 'The Life History of Event Cohorts', ISA Research Conference on Social Stratification, Dublin, April.

Müller, W. and Mayer, K. (1973) *Social Stratification and Career Mobility* (Mouton, The Hague).

Nicholas, A. (1978) *Sociologists in Polytechnics*. SIP Occasional Papers, no. 1, Hatfield.

Nicolaus, M. (1967) 'Proletariat and Middle Class in Marx', *Studies on the Left*, vol. 17, no. 3.

Noble, T. (1972) 'Social Mobility and Class Relations in Britain', *British Journal of Sociology*, vol. 23, no. 4.

Noble, T. (1975a) 'Prolegomena to a Study of Social Mobility and Theories of Social Stratification'. Paper read at the SSRC International Seminar on Social Mobility, Aberdeen, Sep. (mimeo).

Noble, T. (1981) 'Review of Goldthorpe (1980a)' *British Journal of Sociology*, vol. 32, no. 1.

Osipov, G. B. (1969) 'The Class Character of the Theory of Social Mobility', in P. Hollander (ed.) 1969, *American and Soviet Society* (Prentice Hall, Englewood Cliffs).

Pahl, R. (1984) *Divisions of Labour* (Batsford, London).

Pahl, R. and Winkler, J. (1974) 'The Economic Elite', in P. Stanworth and A. Giddens (eds) *Elites and Power in British Society* (Cambridge University Press, London).

Parker, J., Rollet, C. and Jones, K. (1972) 'Health', in A. Halsey (ed.) (1972) *Trends in British Society Since 1900* (Macmillan, London).

Parker, S. R. (1971) *The Effect of the Redundancy Payments Act* (HMSO, London).

Parkin, F. (1971) *Class Inequality and Political Order* (MacGibbon and Kee, London).

Parkin, F. (1979) *Marxism and Class Theory* (Tavistock, London).

Parry, N. and Parry J. (1977) 'Social Control and Collective Social Mobility' in R. Scase (ed.), (1977) *Industrial Society* (Allen and Unwin, London).

Payne, G. (1973a) 'Comparative Sociology: Some Problems of Theory and Method', *British Journal of Sociology*, vol. 24, no. 1.

Payne, G. (1977a) 'Occupation Transition in Advanced Industrial Societies', *Sociological Review*, vol. 25, no. 1.

Payne, G. (1977b) 'Understanding Occupational Transition', *Sociologial Review*, vol. 25, no. 2.

Payne, G. (1987) *Employment and Opportunity* (Macmillan, London).

Payne, G., Ford, G. and Petrie, C. (1975) 'Occupational Mobility in the Scottish Context', Social Science Research Council International Symposium, Aberdeen, Sep.

Payne, G., Ford, G. and Robertson, C. (1976) 'Changes in Occupational Mobility in Scotland', *Scottish Journal of Sociology*, vol. 1, no. 1.

Payne, G., Ford, G. and Robertson, C. (1977) 'A Reappraisal of "Social Mobility in Britain"', *Sociology*, vol. 11, no. 2.

Payne, G. and Ford, G. (1977a) 'Social Mobility in the Upper Echelons', British Sociological Association Conference, Sheffield, March.

Payne, G. and Ford, G. (1977b) 'The Lieutenant Class', *New Society*, vol. 41, no. 772.

Payne, G., Ford, G. and Ulas, M. (1979) *Education and Social Mobility*. SIP Occasional Papers no. 8, Edinburgh.

Payne, G., Ford, G. and Ulas, M. (1980) 'Occupational Change and Social Mobility in Scotland since the First World War', in M. Gaskin (ed.) *The Political Economy of Tolerable Survival* (Croom Helm, London).

Payne, G., Dingwall, R., Payne, J. and Carter, M. (1981) *Sociology and Social Research* (Routledge and Kegan Pual, London).

Payne, G., Payne, J. and Chapman, A. (1983) 'Trends in Female Social Mobility', in E. Gamarnikow, Morgon, D., Purvis, J. and D. Taylorson (eds) *Gender, Class and Work* (Heinemann, London).

Pelling, H. (1963) *A History of British Trade Unionism* (Penguin, Harmondsworth).

Penn, R. (1981) 'The Nuffield Class Categorization', *Sociology*, vol. 15, no. 2.

Penn, R. (1982a) 'Skilled Manual Workers in the Labour Process, 1856–1964', in S. Wood *The Degradation of Work?* (Hutchinson, London).

Penn, R. (1982b) 'Theories of Skill and Class Structure', *Sociological Review*, vol. 3, no. 1.

Perlo, V. (1957) *The Empire of High Finance* (New York, International Publishers).

Piore, M. J. (1975) 'Notes for a Theory of Labour Market Stratification', in R. C. Edwards, M. Reich and D. M. Gordon (eds) *Labour Market Segmentation* (D. C. Heath, Lexington).

Platt, J. (1964) 'Comment on "Social Stratification in Industrial Society"', in P. Halmos (ed.) *The Development of Industrial Societies*, Sociological Review Monograph no. 8 (University of Keele, Keele).

Poulantzas, N. (1973) *Political Power and Social Classes* (New Left Books, London).

Poulantzas, N. (1975) *Classes in Contemporary Capitalism* (New Left Books, London).

Prandy, K., Stewart, A., and Blackburn, R. (1982) *White-Collar Worker* (Macmillan, London).

Raynor, J. (1969) *The Middle Class* (Longmans, London).

Reid, I. (1977) *Social Class Difference in Britain* (1st edn) (Open Books, London).

Reynolds, L. G. (1951) *The Structure of Labour Markets* (Harper, New York).

Richardson, C. J. (1977) *Contemporary Social Mobility.* (Frances Pinter, London).

Ridge, J. (1974a) *Mobility in Britain Reconsidered* (Oxford University Press, Oxford).

Ridge, J. (1974b) 'Sibling Rivalry', in J. Ridge (ed.) (1974) *Mobility in Britain Reconsidered* (Oxford University Press, Oxford).

Ridge, J. and MacDonald, K. (1972) 'Social Mobility', in A. H. Halsey (ed.) *Trends in British Society Since 1900* (Macmillan, London).

Roberts, K. (1978) *The Working Class* (Longmans, London).

Robinson, D. (ed.) (1970) *Local Labour Markets and Wage Structures* (Gower Press, London).

Robinson, R. and Kelley, J. (1979) 'Class as Conceived by Marx and Dahrendorf', *American Sociological Review*, vol. 44, no. 3.

Rogoff, N. (1951) 'Recent Trends in Urban Occupational Mobility', in P. K. Hatt and A. J. Reiss Jnr (eds) (1975) *Cities and Society* (1st edn) (Free Press, Glencoe).

Rollett, C. and Parker, J. (1972) 'Population and Family', in A. H. Halsey (ed.) *Trends in British Society Since 1900* (Macmillan, London).

Rostow, W. (1960) *The Stages of Economic Growth.* (Cambridge University Press, London).

Rothwell, R. and Zegveld, W. (1979) *Technical Change and Employment* (Frances Pinter, London).

Routh, G. (1965) *Occupations and Pay in Great Britain, 1906–60* (Cambridge University Press, Cambridge).

Runciman, W. G. (1966) *Relative Deprivation and Social Justice* (Routledge and Kegan Paul, London).

Salaman, G. (1979) *Work Organisations: Resistance and Control* (Longmans, London).

Sayles, L. R. (1958) *Behaviour of Industrial Work Groups* (Wiley, New York).

Scase, R. (1976) 'A Review of "Class in a Capitalist Society" ', *Sociology*, vol. 10, no. 3.

Scott, J. (1979) *Corporations, Classes and Capitalism* (Hutchinson, London).

Sensini, G. (1913) 'Teoria dell' equilibrio di composizione delle classi sociali', *Rivista Italiana di Sociologia*, Sep./Oct.

Sewell, W. H., Haller, A. D. and Portes, A. (1969) 'The Educational and Early Occupational Attainment Process', *American Sociological Review*, vol. 1, Feb.

Silvey, J. (1975) *Deciphering Data* (Longmans, London).

Singer, P. (1971) 'Forca de Trabalho e Emprego no Brasil 1920–1969', *Cadernos Cebrap Centro Brasileiro de Analise e Planejamento*, vol. 17, Sao Paulo.

Singelmann, J. (1985) 'A Shift/Share Analysis of Industrial and Occupational Change', ESRC Methodology Symposium, Edinburgh, January.

Sjoberg, G. (1951) 'Are Social Classes in America Becoming More Rigid?', *American Sociological Review*, vol. 16, no. 3.

Slaven, A. (1975) *The Development of the West of Scotland, 1750–1960* (Routledge and Kegan Paul, London).

Smith, C. S. (1975) 'The Employment of Sociologists in Research Occupations in Britain in 1973', *Sociology*, vol. 9, No. 2.

Smith, K. B. (1983) 'Class Structure and Intergenerational Mobility from a Marxian Perspective', *Sociology Quarterly*, vol. 22, Summer.

Sombart, W. (1906) *Warum gibt es in den Vereingten Staaten Keinen Socialismus?* (J. C. B. Motir, Tubingen).

Sorokin, P. (1927) *Social Mobility* (Harper, New York).

Stacey, B. (1967) 'Some Psychological Consequences of Intergenerational Mobility', *Human Relations*, vol. 20, no. 1.

Stanworth, P. and Giddens A. (eds) (1974) *Elites and Power in British Society* (Cambridge University Press, London).

Stewart, A., Prandy, K. and Blackburn, R. (1980) *Social Stratification and Occupations* (Macmillan, London).

Strauss, A. L. (1971) *The Contexts of Social Mobility* (Aldine, Chicago).

Svalastoga, K. (1965) 'Social Mobility, The Western European Model, *Acta Sociologica*, vol. 9, no. 2.

Swanson, G. (1971) *Social Change* (Scott, Foresman, Glenview, Ill.).

Touraine, A. (1974) *The Post Industrial Society* (Random House, New York).

Trieman, D. (1970) 'Industrialization and Social Stratification', *Sociological Inquiry1, vol. 40, spring.*

Van Heek, F. (1956) 'Some Introductory Remarks on Social Mobility and Class Structure', in *Transactions of the Third World Congress of Sociology* (ISA, London).

Walker, P. (ed.) (1979) *Between Labour and Class* (Monthly Review Press, New York).

Wallerstein, I. (1974) *The Modern World System* (Academic Press, London).

Weinburg, I. (1969) 'The Problem of the Convergence of Industrial Societies', *Comparative Studies in Society and History*, vol. 11, no. 1.

Wesolowski, W. (1979) *Classes, Strata and Power* (Routledge and Kegan Paul, London).

Westergaard, J. and Resler, H. (1977) *Class in a Capitalist Society* (Penguin, Harmondsworth).

Wood, S. (ed.) (1982) *The Degradation of Work?* (Hutchinson, London).

Woodward, J. (1965) *Industrial Organisation* (Oxford University Press, London).

Worsley, P., Fitzhenry, R., Mitchell, G., Morgan, D., Pons, V., Roberts, B., Sharrock, W. and Ward, R. (1977) *Introducing Sociology* (2nd edn) (Penguin, Harmondsworth).

Wright, E. O. (1976) 'Class Boundaries in Advanced Capitalist Societies', *New Left Review*, vol. 98, July/August.

Wright, E. O. (1978) *Class, Crisis and the State* (New Left Books, London).

Author Index

166

Subject Index

Aberdeen vii, 121
  see also Scottish Mobility Study
accountants 72
ages 82, 106–8, 109, 113, 116, 133, 137, 152
agriculture 54, 60, 69, 83
armed forces 137
attrition rates, class differentials in 109–10
authority 75, 76
automation 64
autonomy 83
average, moving 135–6

banking 32, 33, 67
birth 128, 133
birth-rate 52
Blackcoated Worker, The 150
bourgoisie 23, 36, 39
  petty 22, 40, 41, 44
British Sociological Association 90
brother 105, 114–16
buffer zone 120, 130–1
bureaucratisation 52, 57
bureaucrats 71–2
businessmen, small 22, 120, 125, 126

Cabinet Ministers 132
Capital 34, 39
capital 27, 32, 41, 45, 56–8, 71, 72 73, 81, 136
capitalism 16, 23, 81, 129, 146, 149, 150
capitalism, industrial 32, 55
capitalism, monopoly x, 32, 33, 44, 46, 50, 81
capitalist 32, 38, 40, 49, 58, 71, 72, 75
  see also class, capitalist
capitalist society, theories of 28, 30–51, 59, 68, 71, 73, 146
career 107, 108, 113, 125, 126, 132, 136, 137, 138, 147, 148
Census 16, 21, 47, 48, 94–5, 99, 101, 105, 106, 107, 111, 114, 153
Civil Servants 132
Clapham Report 90, 156
class 86, 115, 120
  and occupational correlates 19–20
  and occupation 19, 41, 49, 50, 66, 71, 72, 73, 75, 76, 87, 147

boundaries 6, 36, 42, 72, 86, 88
capitalist 23, 31–2, 37, 40, 41, 42, 82
conflict 56, 57, 72, 75
consciousness 6, 13, 36, 37, 38, 126
formation 75, 76, 91, 120, 126, 147
hierarchy 119, 132
in D. V. Glass's work 6–8
intermediate 130–1
managerial 44, 45, 101, 103
manual working 75, 98–103, 105–7, 122–3 , 125–7, 129–31, 132, 134, 140, 141
Marxist accounts of 40–46
middle 6, 10, 11, 25, 73, 74, 75, 84, 86–7, 94, 97, 100, 101, 104, 109, 112–13, 127, 130, 132, 147
mobility 14
new middle x, 13, 27, 30, 33, 36, 38, 39, 40–6, 49
non-manual (middle) class 74, 121, 122–3, 125, 127, 128, 129, 131, 135, 137, 144, 152–3
position 20–1, 22
Registrar-General's classification of 98, 99, 105, 111, 124, 153
relations 28, 43, 50, 51, 55, 59, 66, 73, 109
ruling 13, 56, 71
semi-skilled manual 101–3, 123, 126, 128, 131
service 71–2, 75–6
skilled manual 100, 101, 103, 122, 123
situation 21, 127
structure 6, 11, 13, 23, 88, 93, 116, 121–2, 129–132, 148–9
struggle 28, 30, 39, 43, 44, 45, 81, 146
supervisory 101, 103, 123
unskilled manual 101, 103, 123, 126, 128
white-collar 100, 103, 112, 123, 126
working 10, 11, 13, 25, 42, 81, 84, 94, 97, 100, 109, 110, 121, 125, 127, 130, 138, 147
  see also workers, *dritte personen*, recruitment
Class in a Capitalist Society 91, 129–30
clerks 22–3, 33, 39, 42, 48, 130, 153
closure 73, 74, 75, 86, 120, 126, 131
cluster analysis 83

170